ELOU FLEURINE

Rekindling the Spiritual Flame in the Body of Christ

Copyright © 2025 by Elou Fleurine (MBA)

All rights reserved. No part of this publication may be reproduced, distributed, or transmitted in any form or by any means, including photocopying, recording, or other electronic or mechanical methods, without the prior written permission of the author, except in the case of brief quotations embodied in critical reviews and certain other noncommercial uses permitted by copyright law. Permission will be granted upon request.

All Scriptures quotations in the book are from the New King James Version of the Bible. Scripture Quotations marked KJV are taken from King James Version of the Holy Bible. All Greek and Hebrew from the strong Bible Dictionary.

Rekindling the Spiritual Flame in the Body of Christ
For information contact:
Kingjesusuni@gmail.com

1001 NE 15 ST
Homestead, FL 33030
http://www.kingjesush.org

Book and Cover design by JR DESIGNS GROUP FRANCE
ISBN: 978-1-962929-49-3

First Edition: August 2025

Contents

Foreword	iv
Introduction	1
Chapter 1: Understanding the Baptism of Fire	4
Chapter 2: Biblical Foundations of Divine Fire	11
Chapter 3: The Dormant Flame - Diagnosing Spiritual...	20
Chapter 4: Barriers to the Fire	36
Chapter 5: The Process of Rekindling	44
Chapter 6: Walking in the Fire - Daily Spiritual Disciplines	53
Chapter 7: Maintaining the Fire Through Trials	57
Chapter 8: The Fire's Purpose - Mission and Ministry	61
Chapter 9: The Signs of a Fire-Baptized Life	66
Chapter 10: Igniting Others - Passing the Flame	73
Chapter 11: A Church in Fire	86
Conclusion	95
About the Author	99

Foreword

The Church of Jesus Christ stands at a crossroads. In an age of technological advancement and material prosperity, many believers find themselves spiritually cold, going through the motions of faith without the transformative power that once characterized the early Christian community. This book is a clarion call to return to the fire that Jesus promised to baptize us with—a fire that purifies, empowers, and ignites passion for God's kingdom.

As I have walked with God for over two decades in pastoral ministry, I have witnessed both the devastating effects of spiritual lukewarmness and the incredible transformation that occurs when believers encounter the baptism of fire. This work is born from a burden to see the Body of Christ rekindled with divine passion and power.

The pages that follow are not merely theoretical discussions but practical pathways to spiritual renewal. They represent years of biblical study, pastoral experience, and personal encounters with the refining fire of God. My prayer is that as you read these words, the Holy Spirit will fan the flames of your heart and ignite a fire that will never be extinguished.

Introduction

The Call to Spiritual Fire

"I baptize you with water for repentance. But after me comes one who is more powerful than I, whose sandals I am not worthy to carry. He will baptize you with the Holy Spirit and fire." - Matthew 3:11

The words of John the Baptist echo through the centuries, carrying a promise that has the power to revolutionize our spiritual lives. Jesus Christ, the One who is more powerful, offers us a baptism unlike any other—a baptism with the Holy Spirit and fire. This divine fire is not merely a metaphor; it is a spiritual reality that transforms hearts, empowers service, and ignites passion for the things of God.

Yet, as we survey the contemporary Christian landscape, we must ask ourselves: Where is this fire? Why do so many believers live defeated, powerless lives? Why do our churches often resemble social clubs more than houses of prayer? Why has the fire that once turned the world upside down seemingly been reduced to mere embers in many hearts?

The answer lies not in God's unwillingness to baptize us with fire, but in our failure to understand, seek, and maintain this divine flame. The fire of God is as available today as it was on the Day of Pentecost, but it requires hearts that are prepared, hungry, and willing to be consumed by His presence.

The Current State of the Church

As I travel and minister in various churches, I observe a troubling pattern. Many believers have settled for a form of godliness that lacks power. They know the right words, sing the right songs, and perform the right rituals, but their lives lack the transformative fire that should characterize every follower of Christ.

This spiritual lukewarmness manifests in several ways:

Prayerless Christianity: Prayer meetings are sparsely attended. Personal prayer lives are sporadic at best. The very activity that connects us to the source of all power is neglected.

Powerless Witnessing: Despite the Great Commission, many believers rarely share their faith. When they do, it often lacks conviction and power, resulting in minimal impact.

Comfort-Seeking Faith: Rather than seeking God's will and purposes, many believers use faith as a means to achieve personal comfort and success.

Divided Communities: Churches split over minor issues while major spiritual battles are ignored. The unity that Jesus prayed for seems elusive.

Moral Compromise: The line between the church and the world has become increasingly blurred, with many believers living by worldly standards rather than biblical principles.

These symptoms point to a deeper problem: the absence of the baptism of fire in the lives of believers and in our corporate gatherings.

The Promise of Transformation

However, this book is not written in despair but in hope. The same God who breathed upon the dry bones in Ezekiel's vision is ready to breathe upon His church today. The same fire that fell on Mount Carmel, that descended at Pentecost, and that has ignited revivals throughout church history is available to every believer who will seek it with all their heart.

The baptism of fire is not reserved for a select few spiritual elites. It is the birthright of every born-again believer. It is not a one-time experience but a continuous lifestyle of being filled, refilled, and consumed by God's presence.

What This Book Will Do

INTRODUCTION

This book will guide you through a biblical understanding of the baptism of fire and provide practical steps to experience and maintain this divine flame in your life. We will explore:

- The biblical foundations of divine fire
- How to recognize spiritual lukewarmness in our lives
- The barriers that prevent us from experiencing God's fire
- Practical steps to prepare our hearts for divine ignition
- How to maintain the fire through challenges and trials
- The purpose and mission of a fire-baptized life
- How to help others experience this same transformation

Each chapter builds upon the previous one, creating a comprehensive roadmap for spiritual renewal. The goal is not merely to gain knowledge but to experience transformation—to move from spiritual mediocrity to passionate discipleship.

A Personal Invitation

As you begin this journey, I want to extend a personal invitation. Don't simply read these pages as an academic exercise. Allow the Holy Spirit to search your heart, to reveal areas of spiritual dryness, and to kindle fresh hunger for more of God.

The fire of God is both wonderful and terrible, comforting and consuming, gentle and powerful. It will transform every area of your life—your relationships, your priorities, your ministry, and your destiny. Are you ready for such a transformation?

The journey begins with a simple prayer: "Lord, baptize me with Your fire."

Chapter 1: Understanding the Baptism of Fire

"*He will baptize you with the Holy Spirit and fire.*" - Matthew 3:11

To embark on the journey toward spiritual renewal, we must first understand what the baptism of fire truly means. This concept, introduced by John the Baptist and fulfilled through Jesus Christ, represents one of the most powerful spiritual realities available to believers. Yet, it is also one of the most misunderstood doctrines in contemporary Christianity.

The concept of "Baptism of Fire" has long been a powerful and transformative idea within Christian theology. It represents a profound spiritual experience that goes beyond the physical act of water baptism, signifying a deeper immersion into the Holy Spirit's power and presence.

To truly grasp the essence of the Baptism of Fire, we must first explore its biblical roots. The phrase originates from the words of John the Baptist in Matthew 3:11, where he declares, "I baptize you with water for repentance, but he who is coming after me is mightier than I, whose sandals I am not worthy to carry. He will baptize you with the Holy Spirit and fire."

This prophetic statement points to Jesus Christ as the one who would bring about a spiritual baptism far more potent than the water baptism John performed. The imagery of fire is significant, symbolizing purification, passion, and power.

The Baptism of Fire is often associated with the day of Pentecost, as

CHAPTER 1: UNDERSTANDING THE BAPTISM OF FIRE

described in Acts 2:1-4. On this day, the disciples were filled with the Holy Spirit, and "tongues of fire" appeared to rest on each of them. This event marked the beginning of the early Christian church and demonstrated the transformative power of the Holy Spirit.

But what does the Baptism of Fire mean for believers today? It represents a radical renewal of faith, a rekindling of spiritual fervor, and a deeper connection with God. It's not merely an emotional experience, but a profound encounter that leads to lasting change and empowerment for Christian service.

Key aspects of the Baptism of Fire include:

1. Purification: Just as fire refines precious metals, the Baptism of Fire purifies believers, burning away impurities and strengthening faith.
2. Passion: It ignites a renewed zeal for God and His purposes, inspiring believers to live out their faith with enthusiasm.
3. Power: The Baptism of Fire empowers Christians to live boldly for Christ, equipped with spiritual gifts for ministry and evangelism.
4. Presence: It brings a heightened awareness of God's presence and a deeper intimacy in one's relationship with Him.

As we delve deeper into this book, we'll explore how to prepare for, experience, and live out the reality of the Baptism of Fire in our lives and communities. It's a journey of spiritual awakening that has the potential to transform not only individual believers but also the entire Body of Christ.

In the following chapters, we'll examine biblical examples, share contemporary testimonies, and provide practical guidance for those seeking this powerful spiritual experience. Our goal is to help rekindle the spiritual flame within the Church, igniting a revival that will impact our world for Christ.

Remember, the Baptism of Fire is not a one-time event, but an ongoing process of yielding to the Holy Spirit's work in our lives. As we open ourselves to this divine fire, we position ourselves for continual growth, renewal, and effectiveness in our Christian walk.

Defining the Baptism of Fire

The Greek word for baptism, "baptizo," means to immerse, to plunge, or to overwhelm completely. When John spoke of Jesus baptizing with fire, he was describing a complete immersion in the divine nature and power of God. This is not a surface experience or a momentary feeling; it is a complete transformation that affects every aspect of our being.

Fire, throughout Scripture, represents several divine attributes:

Purification: Fire burns away impurities, leaving only what is valuable and pure. In the spiritual realm, God's fire purifies our hearts, motives, and desires.

Power: Fire is one of nature's most powerful forces. Spiritually, it represents the unlimited power of God working through surrendered lives.

Presence: Fire provides light in darkness and warmth in cold. God's fire represents His manifest presence in our lives and communities.

Passion: Fire burns with intensity and cannot be ignored. The baptism of fire ignites passionate love for God and His purposes.

Judgment: Fire consumes what is worthless while refining what is valuable. God's fire burns away sin while strengthening righteousness.

When we speak of the baptism of fire, we are describing a spiritual experience where God's presence overwhelms our lives, purifying our hearts, empowering our service, and igniting passionate devotion to Him.

Biblical Precedents

The concept of divine fire is woven throughout Scripture, from the Old Testament to the New Testament. Understanding these precedents helps us appreciate the full significance of Jesus' promise to baptize with fire.

Moses and the Burning Bush (Exodus 3:1-6): When Moses encountered God in the burning bush, he witnessed fire that burned without consuming. This supernatural fire represented God's holy presence and His call to Moses for service. The fire transformed Moses from a shepherd into a deliverer.

Mount Sinai (Exodus 19:16-18): When God descended upon Mount Sinai to give the Law, the mountain was covered with fire, smoke, and earthquake. This dramatic display of God's fiery presence established His authority and holiness before the entire nation of Israel.

Elijah on Mount Carmel (1 Kings 18:36-39): When Elijah challenged the prophets of Baal, fire fell from heaven and consumed the sacrifice, the wood, the stones, and even the water. This divine fire vindicated God's power and turned the hearts of the people back to Him.

Isaiah's Cleansing (Isaiah 6:6-7): When Isaiah saw the Lord in His temple, a seraph touched his lips with a live coal from the altar, cleansing him from sin and preparing him for prophetic ministry. The fire of God purified and commissioned Isaiah for service.

Pentecost (Acts 2:1-4): On the Day of Pentecost, tongues of fire appeared above the heads of the disciples, and they were filled with the Holy Spirit. This baptism of fire empowered them for worldwide ministry and launched the Christian church.

These biblical accounts demonstrate that God's fire is not merely symbolic but represents real, transformative encounters with divine power and presence.

The Distinction Between Water Baptism and Fire Baptism

John the Baptist clearly distinguished between his baptism with water and Jesus' baptism with the Holy Spirit and fire. This distinction is crucial for understanding the fullness of Christian experience.

Water Baptism represents:

- Repentance from sin
- Death to the old life
- Public declaration of faith
- Initial cleansing
- Identification with Christ's death and resurrection

Fire Baptism represents:

- Empowerment for service
- Purification of heart and motive
- Passionate devotion to God
- Supernatural gifting
- Continuous filling and refilling

While water baptism is a one-time event that occurs at the beginning of our Christian journey, the baptism of fire is both an initial experience and an ongoing lifestyle. We can be baptized with fire multiple times as we surrender deeper areas of our lives to God's transforming power.

The Role of the Holy Spirit

The baptism of fire cannot be separated from the person and work of the Holy Spirit. Jesus promised that He would send the Holy Spirit as our Helper, Comforter, and Guide. The fire of God is not an impersonal force but the very presence of the Holy Spirit working in and through our lives.

The Holy Spirit's fire manifests in several ways:

Conviction: The Spirit's fire brings conviction of sin, righteousness, and judgment, leading to repentance and transformation.

Illumination: The fire of the Spirit enlightens our understanding of God's Word and His will for our lives.

Empowerment: The Spirit's fire gives us supernatural ability to live holy lives and serve effectively in ministry.

Gifting: The baptism of fire releases spiritual gifts that enable us to minister with divine power and effectiveness.

Intercession: The Spirit's fire ignites fervent prayer and intercession, connecting us with God's heart and purposes.

Common Misconceptions

Several misconceptions about the baptism of fire have hindered believers from experiencing this transformative reality:

Misconception 1: It's Only for Special People

Some believe that the baptism of fire is reserved for pastors, missionaries, or other "spiritual elites." This is false. Every believer has access to this experience because it is part of our inheritance in Christ.

Misconception 2: It's a One-Time Event

While there may be initial moments of fire baptism, it is not a one-time experience. We need continuous filling and refilling as we face new challenges and surrender deeper areas of our lives.

Misconception 3: It's Purely Emotional

Some dismiss the baptism of fire as mere emotionalism. While emotions may be involved, this experience is fundamentally about spiritual transformation and empowerment, not just feelings.

Misconception 4: It's Automatic

The baptism of fire is not automatic upon salvation. It requires hunger, seeking, and surrender. Many believers miss this experience because they don't actively pursue it.

Misconception 5: It Guarantees Perfection

Fire baptism doesn't make us perfect or eliminate all struggles. It does, however, provide power to overcome sin and live victoriously.

The Fruit of Fire Baptism

When believers experience genuine baptism of fire, certain characteristics become evident in their lives:

Boldness in Witness: Fear of sharing the gospel is replaced with supernatural courage and effectiveness in evangelism.

Passion for Prayer: Prayer becomes a delight rather than a duty. Time in God's presence becomes the highlight of each day.

Love for God's Word: Scripture comes alive with fresh revelation and personal application. Bible study becomes exciting and transformative.

Holiness: Sin loses its appeal as the beauty of Christ becomes more attractive. Righteousness becomes natural rather than forced.

Compassion for Others: Hearts break for what breaks God's heart. Ministry to hurting people becomes a joyful privilege.

Unity in the Body: Petty differences fade as believers focus on their common mission and shared love for Christ.

Expectancy for Miracles: Faith rises to expect God to move supernaturally in response to prayer and ministry.

Preparing for the Journey

Understanding the baptism of fire is just the beginning. The remaining chapters of this book will guide you through the practical steps of experiencing and maintaining this divine flame in your life. But understanding is crucial because it provides the foundation for everything that follows.

As we conclude this first chapter, take time to examine your own spiritual condition. Are you satisfied with your current level of spiritual experience? Do you hunger for more of God's presence and power in your life? Are you willing to pay the price for genuine spiritual transformation?

The baptism of fire is not for the casual Christian who wants just enough of God to feel secure but not enough to be transformed. It is for those who are desperate for genuine encounter with the living God, who are willing to be consumed by His love, and who desire to be vessels of His power in a needy world.

The fire of God is available. The question is: Are you ready to be baptized with fire?

Chapter 2: Biblical Foundations of Divine Fire

"*For our God is a consuming fire.*" - Hebrews 12:29

To fully understand and experience the baptism of fire, we must establish solid biblical foundations. Scripture provides numerous accounts of divine fire and its transformative power. These biblical precedents not only validate the authenticity of fire baptism but also provide patterns for how God works through His fire today.

The concept of divine fire is deeply rooted in Scripture, appearing throughout both the Old and New Testaments as a powerful symbol of God's presence, purification, and power. In this chapter, we'll explore key biblical passages that establish the foundation for understanding the Baptism of Fire.

The Nature of Divine Fire in Scripture

Divine fire in the Bible is multifaceted, representing various aspects of God's character and interaction with humanity:

a) Holiness: Fire often symbolizes God's absolute holiness and the purifying effect it has on those who encounter Him (Isaiah 6:1-7).

b) Presence: From the burning bush to the pillar of fire, divine fire signifies God's tangible presence among His people (Exodus 3:2-4, 13:21-22).

c) Power: Fire demonstrates God's overwhelming power and authority (1 Kings 18:38-39).

d) Judgment: Divine fire can represent God's righteous judgment against sin (Genesis 19:24-25, Revelation 20:14-15).

e) Purification: The refiner's fire metaphor illustrates God's purifying work in believers' lives (Malachi 3:2-3).

```
Old Testament References:
```

The Burning Bush (Exodus 3:1-6): God first appeared to Moses in the form of a burning bush that was not consumed. This miraculous fire represented God's holiness and His calling upon Moses' life.

- Signifies God's self-revelation and calling.
- Demonstrates God's ability to manifest His presence without consuming the natural order.

The Pillar of Fire (Exodus 13:21-22): During the Exodus, God led the Israelites by a pillar of fire at night, symbolizing His guidance and protection.

- Represents God's guidance and protection.
- Illustrates God's constant presence with His people.

The Mount Sinai (Exodus 19:18): When God descended on Mount Sinai, the mountain was covered in smoke "because the Lord had descended on it in fire."

Perhaps no Old Testament account better demonstrates the power of divine fire than Elijah's confrontation with the prophets of Baal. After the false prophets failed to bring fire from their god, Elijah's simple prayer brought immediate response:

CHAPTER 2: BIBLICAL FOUNDATIONS OF DIVINE FIRE

- The fire consumed the sacrifice
- The fire consumed the wood and stones
- The fire consumed the water in the trench
- The fire vindicated God's power
- The fire turned the people's hearts back to God

This account establishes important principles about divine fire:

- It responds to faith-filled prayer
- It demonstrates God's superiority over false gods
- It has power to transform hearts
- It brings glory to God alone
- It emphasizes the awe-inspiring nature of God's presence
- It sets the stage for the giving of the Law

Elijah and the Prophets of Baal (1 Kings 18:20-40): God demonstrated His power through fire, consuming Elijah's water-drenched sacrifice.

- Proves God's supremacy over false gods
- Demonstrates the power of true faith

Isaiah's Vision (Isaiah 6:1-7): When Isaiah saw the Lord in His temple, he was overwhelmed by his own sinfulness. A seraph took a live coal from the altar and touched Isaiah's lips, declaring his guilt removed and sin atoned for. This fire accomplished:

- Conviction of sin
- Cleansing from guilt
- Commissioning for service
- Preparation for ministry
- Reveals the purifying nature of God's presence

- Illustrates the preparation required for divine service

New Testament Foundations:

The New Testament builds upon Old Testament foundations while revealing new dimensions of divine fire through the person and work of Jesus Christ.

John the Baptist introduced the concept of fire baptism, distinguishing it from water baptism. He prophesied that Jesus would baptize with the Holy Spirit and fire, accomplishing both purification and empowerment. John also mentioned the fire of judgment that would burn up the chaff, indicating fire's dual purpose of blessing the righteous and judging the wicked.

a) John the Baptist's Prophecy (Matthew 3:11-12, Luke 3:16-17): John foretold that Jesus would baptize with the Holy Spirit and fire, introducing the concept of spiritual baptism.

b) Pentecost (Acts 2:1-4): The Holy Spirit descended upon the disciples as "tongues of fire," marking the birth of the Church.

c) Refiner's Fire (Malachi 3:2-3, 1 Peter 1:7): These passages use the metaphor of refining fire to describe God's purifying work in believers' lives.

Symbolic Meanings of Fire in Scripture:

a) God's Presence: Fire often signifies God's manifest presence (Exodus 19:18, Acts 2:3).

b) Purification: Fire represents the purifying work of God in believers' lives (Isaiah 6:6-7, Zechariah 13:9).

c) Judgment: Divine fire can also symbolize God's judgment (Genesis 19:24, 2 Peter 3:7).

CHAPTER 2: BIBLICAL FOUNDATIONS OF DIVINE FIRE

d) Passion and Zeal: Fire depicts the fervor and enthusiasm for God's work (Jeremiah 20:9, Luke 24:32).

Jesus and Fire:

Jesus declared, "I have come to bring fire on the earth, and how I wish it were already kindled!" This passionate statement reveals Christ's intense desire to see divine fire released on earth. He understood that His death and resurrection would open the way for this fire to be poured out on all flesh. When Jesus was transfigured before Peter, James, and John, His face shone like the sun and His clothes became white as light. While not explicitly called fire, this divine radiance represents the same glory-fire that will characterize believers when they are fully transformed.

a) Luke 12:49: Jesus states, "I have come to bring fire on the earth, and how I wish it were already kindled!"

b) Revelation 1:14: In John's vision, Jesus' eyes are described as "like blazing fire."

The Holy Spirit and Fire:

The Day of Pentecost marks the fulfillment of Jesus' promise to baptize with the Holy Spirit and fire. The tongues of fire that appeared above each disciple's head were visible manifestations of invisible spiritual reality. This fire baptism resulted in:

- Supernatural boldness
- Effective communication across language barriers
- Immediate church growth
- Powerful preaching
- Signs and wonders
- Unity among believers

a) Acts 2:3-4: The Holy Spirit's arrival at Pentecost is marked by "tongues of fire."

b) Romans 12:11: Believers are encouraged to keep their "spiritual fervor."

The Refining Process:

1 Corinthians 3:13-15: Our works will be tested by fire. b) 1 Peter 4:12: Trials are described as a "fiery ordeal."

Understanding these biblical foundations is crucial for grasping the full significance of the Baptism of Fire. This divine fire is not just a New Testament concept but is woven throughout the entire biblical narrative. It represents God's presence, His purifying work, and the empowerment He provides to His people.

As we continue to explore the Baptism of Fire, we'll see how these biblical themes of divine fire apply to our lives today. The same God who appeared to Moses in the burning bush, who sent fire from heaven for Elijah, and who filled the disciples at Pentecost, desires to ignite a holy fire in the hearts of believers today.

Paul's Burning Heart (2 Corinthians 11:28-29)

Paul described the daily pressure of his concern for all the churches and asked, "Who is weak, and I do not feel weak? Who is led into sin, and I do not inwardly burn?" This burning represents the fire of pastoral concern and godly jealousy that consumes those baptized with divine fire.

The Refiner's Fire (1 Corinthians 3:10-15)

Paul used the metaphor of fire testing each person's work to determine its quality. Gold, silver, and precious stones survive the fire, while wood, hay, and stubble are consumed. This teaching reveals fire's refining purpose in believers' lives.

God as Consuming Fire (Hebrews 12:29)

The writer of Hebrews declares that "our God is a consuming fire," emphasizing that God's essential nature includes this fiery aspect. This consuming fire burns away everything that hinders our relationship with Him while preserving and strengthening what is valuable.

Symbolic Meanings of Biblical Fire

Throughout Scripture, fire carries consistent symbolic meanings that help us understand the baptism of fire:

Purification

Fire removes impurities from precious metals, and God's fire removes sin and worldliness from believers' hearts. This purification is often uncomfortable but always beneficial.

Testing

Fire reveals the quality of materials, and spiritual fire reveals the authenticity of our faith and works. Only what has eternal value survives divine testing.

Judgment

Fire consumes what is worthless, and God's fire burns away sin, rebellion, and everything that opposes His kingdom. This aspect of fire should create holy reverence.

Empowerment

Fire provides energy and power, and spiritual fire energizes believers for effective service and ministry. This empowerment enables supernatural accomplishments.

Passion

Fire burns with intensity, and divine fire ignites passionate love for God, His Word, His people, and His purposes. This passion sustains believers through difficulties.

Presence

Fire provides light and warmth, and God's fire represents His manifest presence among His people. This presence brings comfort, guidance, and assurance.

Protection

Fire can ward off enemies, and spiritual fire provides divine protection against spiritual attacks and opposition. Believers walking in God's fire are surrounded by His power.

Patterns for Modern Experience

The biblical accounts of divine fire establish patterns that remain relevant for contemporary believers:

Fire Comes to the Prepared

Biblical characters who experienced divine fire were prepared through prayer, fasting, obedience, and surrender. God's fire doesn't fall on unprepared hearts.

Fire Follows Faith

Divine fire responds to faith-filled prayer and expectation. Those who doubt or approach God casually rarely experience His fire.

Fire Brings Transformation

Every biblical fire encounter resulted in transformation—changed lives, renewed purpose, and increased effectiveness. Fire baptism isn't merely an experience; it's a transformation.

Fire Requires Maintenance

The tabernacle fire was to burn continually, requiring constant attention and fuel. Similarly, the fire of God in our lives requires ongoing cultivation through spiritual disciplines.

Fire Has Purpose

Biblical fire always accomplished specific purposes—purification, empowerment, guidance, or judgment. God's fire in our lives has definite purposes that we must understand and cooperate with.

Preparing for Personal Fire Encounters

Based on biblical patterns, several principles emerge for those seeking baptism of fire:

Cultivate Holy Hunger

Every biblical character who experienced divine fire had intense hunger for God. This hunger cannot be manufactured but develops through recognition of our spiritual need.

Embrace Holiness

God's fire is holy fire. Those who would host His presence must pursue holiness in thought, word, and deed. Sin quenches the Spirit's fire.

Develop Faith Expectancy

Biblical fire encounters required faith that expected God to move. Doubt and unbelief hinder the flow of divine fire.

Practice Surrender

Fire consumes what it touches. Those seeking God's fire must be willing to be consumed—to have their agendas, desires, and plans transformed by His purposes.

Maintain Spiritual Disciplines

Prayer, fasting, Bible study, and worship create atmospheric conditions conducive to divine fire. These disciplines don't earn God's fire but prepare us to receive it.

The biblical foundations clearly establish that divine fire is not an antiquated concept but a present reality available to every believer. The same God who appeared in the burning bush, who consumed Elijah's sacrifice, and who filled the disciples at Pentecost desires to baptize contemporary believers with His fire.

As we move forward in our study, these biblical foundations will serve as our reference point for understanding how God's fire operates in modern believers' lives. The principles established in Scripture remain unchanged, even though the specific manifestations may vary according to God's purposes and our needs.

In the next chapter, we'll examine how this biblical understanding of divine fire translates into practical experiences of spiritual renewal and empowerment in the lives of contemporary believers.

Chapter 3: The Dormant Flame - Diagnosing Spiritual Lukewarmness

"*I know your deeds, that you are neither cold nor hot. I wish you were either one or the other! So, because you are lukewarm—neither hot nor cold—I am about to spit you out of my mouth.*" - Revelation 3:15-16

Before we can experience the baptism of fire, we must honestly assess our current spiritual condition. The church at Laodicea provides a sobering example of believers who had become spiritually lukewarm—a condition that Jesus found repulsive. Understanding the symptoms, causes, and consequences of spiritual lukewarmness is essential for anyone seeking genuine spiritual renewal.

This chapter explores the nature of spiritual apathy, its causes, and how to recognize it in our lives.

Understanding Spiritual Lukewarmness:

a) Biblical Reference: Revelation 3:15-16 "I know your deeds, that you are neither cold nor hot. I wish you were either one or the other! So, because you are lukewarm—neither hot nor cold, I am about to spit you out of my mouth."

b) Definition: Spiritual lukewarmness is a state of indifference or half-hardheartedness in one's relationship with God. It's characterized by a lack of passion, commitment, and spiritual vitality.

CHAPTER 3: THE DORMANT FLAME - DIAGNOSING SPIRITUAL...

The Lukewarm Church refers to a body of believers—or an individual Christian—who is spiritually indifferent, complacent, and lacking genuine passion or commitment to God. It describes a condition where faith exists in name, but lacks depth, zeal, or full obedience.

They are not cold (hostile to God), nor hot (on fire for God)—but in a neutral, self-satisfied state that deceives them into thinking they're spiritually well, when in fact, they're spiritually poor.

Signs of Spiritual Lukewarmness:

a) Lack of Enthusiasm in Worship and Prayer - A noticeable decrease in passion, engagement, and joy during times of worship and prayer, often characterized by going through the motions without heart involvement.

A lack of enthusiasm in worship and prayer is often one of the first and most noticeable signs of spiritual lukewarmness. By identifying this issue, believers can take proactive steps to address the underlying causes and seek renewed fervor in their relationship with God. This recognition sets the stage for a deeper experience of the Baptism of Fire, which promises to reignite passion and restore the joy of intimate communion with God.

b) Inconsistent Bible Study and Meditation - An irregular and sporadic approach to engaging with Scripture, characterized by a lack of depth, consistency, and intentional reflection on God's Word. The example of Solis, a busy professional and father of two, exemplifies inconsistent Bible study and meditation:

Monday: Solis intends to start a new Bible reading plan but gets caught up in work emails.

Tuesday: He reads a quick devotional on his phone app during his commute but doesn't open his Bible.

Wednesday: Feeling guilty, Solis reads three chapters of Psalms before bed but falls asleep midway.

Thursday: No Bible reading; Solis tells himself he'll catch up on the weekend.

Friday: Solis listens to a Christian podcast during his workout, considering it a substitute for Bible study.

Saturday: Busy with family activities, Solis forgets about Bible reading entirely.

Sunday: At church, Solis realizes he's unfamiliar with the passage being preached. He resolves to be more consistent but isn't sure how to start.

This pattern repeats week after week, leaving Solis feeling disconnected from God's Word and unsure of how to break the cycle.

Inconsistent Bible study and meditation is a clear indicator of spiritual lukewarmness. By identifying this issue and taking intentional steps to establish regular, meaningful engagement with Scripture, believers can reignite their passion for God's Word. This renewed commitment sets the stage for a deeper experience of the Baptism of Fire, which promises to ignite a lasting hunger for Scripture and the wisdom to apply it in daily life.

c) Diminished Desire for Fellowship with Other Believers - A noticeable decrease in the eagerness to engage, connect, and spend time with other Christians, often characterized by isolation, reduced church attendance, and minimal participation in faith-based community activities.

d) Decreased Sensitivity to Sin- A reduction in one's awareness, conviction, and repentance towards sin, often characterized by a gradual normalization or justification of behaviors that were previously recognized as contrary to biblical principles.

e) Complacency in Spiritual Growth- A state of contentment or satisfaction with one's current spiritual condition, characterized by a lack of intentionality, urgency, and active pursuit of continued growth in Christ.

f) Absence of Spiritual Hunger and Thirst - The lack of a deep, insatiable desire for a closer relationship with God, characterized by a diminished longing for spiritual nourishment, revelation, and intimate communion with the divine.

A young lady had been a committed Christian for nearly five years at KJUM, actively involved in the church. In her early years of faith, she had been passionate about her relationship with God, spending regular time in prayer and Bible study, opened her home for House of Peace. She had a deep longing to know Him more and see His work in her life.

However, over time, her spiritual fervor began to wane. The demands of her needs, social life, and other commitments gradually crowded out the priority she once placed on nurturing her relationship with the Lord.

Instead of eagerly participating her weekly house of peace, She found herself rushing through it, often distracted and unfocused. She would occasionally skip her quiet time altogether, justifying it by saying she was "too busy" or "too tired."

During worship services at the church, she would find her mind wandering, her attention drifting away from the lyrics and messages. She no longer experienced the same sense of awe and reverence that had once characterized her worship.

When her mentor would suggest discussing a challenging theological topic or sharing prayer requests, she would often remain silent, preferring to avoid the deeper spiritual conversations. She found herself less and less interested in exploring the riches of God's Word or wrestling with the complexities of her faith.

Over time, her passion for spiritual growth had diminished to the point where she felt content with her current level of spiritual maturity and preferred to watch the service online. She no longer felt a deep, consuming thirst for more of God, a longing that had once driven her to seek Him wholeheartedly. As the result, she lost her business and left the ministry.

This absence of spiritual hunger and thirst was a clear sign of her lukewarm spiritual condition. She recognized that her relationship with

God had become stagnant, and she knew she needed to take steps to reignite her passion and desire for the Lord. Yet, the inertia of her complacency made it difficult for her to take that first step.

Her story serves as a sobering reminder of the importance of maintaining a vibrant, insatiable spiritual appetite. When we lose our hunger and thirst for God, we risk becoming spiritually stagnant and ineffective in our walk with Him.

g) Prioritizing Worldly Pursuits over Spiritual Matters - This refers to a state where an individual places a greater emphasis and focus on temporal, earthly concerns and activities over the pursuit of spiritual growth, kingdom advancement, and eternal matters.

The Rich Young Ruler The story of the rich young ruler in Matthew 19:16-22 provides a poignant example of someone who prioritized his worldly possessions over following Jesus. Despite his outward religious observance, he was unwilling to surrender his wealth and status, ultimately choosing the temporary over the eternal.

h) Lack of Evangelistic Zeal - The absence of a fervent, Christ-centered desire to share the gospel and see others come to a saving knowledge of Jesus. This is characterized by a diminished urgency, passion, and intentionality in evangelistic efforts.

The Parable of the Lost Sheep In Luke 15:3-7, Jesus tells the parable of the shepherd who leaves the ninety-nine sheep to search for the one that is lost. This powerful illustration highlights the heart of God for the salvation of the lost and the urgency that should characterize the believer's evangelistic efforts.

Causes of Spiritual Lukewarmness

- Unresolved Sin and Guilt - Unresolved sin and guilt refers to the presence of unconfessed, unrepented, or unresolved sin in a believer's life, which leads to a persistent sense of guilt, shame, and spiritual discomfort. This spiritual condition is characterized by the failure to fully acknowledge, confront, and experience God's forgiveness and restoration regarding specific sins or areas of disobedience.

"If we confess our sins, he is faithful and just and will forgive us our sins and purify us from all unrighteousness." (1 John 1:9) This verse underscores the promise of God's forgiveness and restoration for those who confess their sins, highlighting the importance of addressing unresolved sin and guilt.

- Spiritual Wounds or Disappointments - Spiritual wounds or disappointments refer to deep emotional and psychological scars that a believer has experienced within the context of their spiritual journey, often leading to a diminished sense of trust, security, and enthusiasm in their relationship with God.
- Busyness and Distractions of Life - Busyness and distractions of life refer to the overwhelming demands, activities, and preoccupations that consume a believer's time and attention, often to the detriment of their spiritual vitality and focus. This condition is characterized by a believer's inability to maintain a healthy balance between the temporal and the eternal, leading to a neglect of their relationship with God and their spiritual growth.

Alcanta, a dedicated leader in the ministry, found herself caught in a whirlwind of activities and responsibilities. She worked long hours at her job, started very well on a committee at KJUM, and was heavily involved in the church activities. While Alcanta's intentions were good, she soon realized that her schedule had become overwhelming, leaving her little time for personal devotion, prayer, and meaningful fellowship with other believers.

Alcanta's spiritual life began to suffer as she found herself constantly tired, stressed, and disconnected from God. She struggled to maintain a consistent quiet time and often felt guilty for neglecting her relationship with the Lord and serving the committee she was called to. Alcanta's busyness had become a distraction, preventing her from experiencing the depth of intimacy and spiritual growth she once had. Recognizing the need for change, Alcanta began to re-evaluate her priorities, set boundaries, and make intentional efforts to create more margin in her life for God and spiritual nourishment.

- Lack of Spiritual Disciplines - Lack of spiritual disciplines refers to the absence or neglect of regular spiritual practices that are essential for the believer's ongoing growth, renewal, and intimacy with God. This condition is characterized by a believer's failure to consistently engage in activities such as prayer, Bible reading, meditation, fasting, and other spiritual disciplines that facilitate a vibrant relationship with Christ.

The lack of spiritual disciplines hinders the believer's ability to develop a deep, personal relationship with God, leading to a sense of spiritual distance and dryness.

- Stagnation in Spiritual Growth: Without the consistent practice of spiritual disciplines, the believer's spiritual maturity and transformation are stunted, preventing them from reaching their full potential in Christ.
- Gradual Drift from Initial Passion - The gradual drift from initial passion refers to the slow and often unnoticed decline in enthusiasm, commitment, or emotional connection to a goal, purpose, relationship, or calling that once deeply inspired or motivated you.

The Church in Ephesus (Revelation 2:4): "Yet I hold this against you:

You have forsaken the love you had at first."

Jesus praises the Ephesian church for their hard work and perseverance but rebukes them for losing their first love—their initial passion for Him.

Despite doing "good things," their heart was no longer fully engaged. It's a classic picture of how duty can replace devotion when passion drifts.

Kemi was once a passionate worship leader in KJU Ministry. He arrived early for prayer, sought God earnestly, and led with authenticity that moved hearts. People could see—and feel—that he worshiped from a deep place.

But over the years, things changed.

- He began selecting songs based on trends, not spiritual discernment.
- Prayer before service became optional—or rushed.
- He stopped seeking God during the week, only preparing "on Saturday night."
- He still had the voice, the talent, and the role—but the **anointing had faded**, replaced by performance and routine.

The Dangers of Remaining Lukewarm

A lukewarm Christian is half-hearted—claiming faith but living in compromise. They:

- Attend church but resist transformation (James 1:22).
- Pray occasionally but ignore God's Word daily (Hosea 4:6).
- Serve when convenient but avoid sacrifice (Luke 9:23).

Example:

The church of Laodicea (Revelation 3:14-22) was wealthy but spiritually bankrupt. Jesus rebuked them for trusting in riches while neglecting their need for Him.

a) Ineffectiveness in Christian Witness - Ineffectiveness in Christian witness refers to a believer's failure to authentically reflect Christ or impact others for the Kingdom due to compromise, hypocrisy, or spiritual apathy. It is marked by a disconnect between professed faith and practical living, rendering testimony powerless

b) Vulnerability to Temptation and Spiritual Attacks - Vulnerability to temptation and spiritual attacks refers to a weakened spiritual state that makes a believer more susceptible to sin, demonic influence, or discouragement.

Vulnerability to temptation and spiritual attacks refers to a weakened state of mind, spirit, or discipline in which a person becomes more susceptible to falling into sin, doubt, or deception—often due to fatigue, isolation, disobedience, pride, or distance from God.

It's when your spiritual defenses are down, making it easier for the enemy to influence your thoughts, decisions, or emotions.

This occurs when:

- Spiritual defenses are down (neglecting prayer, Scripture, accountability).
- Unresolved sin or strongholds exist (Ephesians 4:27; James 1:14–15).
- Emotional or physical exhaustion sets in (1 Peter 5:8).

Lidia used to start teaching House of Peace every Wednesday. But lately, life got busy—early work, family stress, no time for devotion. She told herself, *"I'll get back to it when things calm down."*

Days turned into weeks.

She became irritable, insecure, and quietly distant from God.

Then an old temptation reappeared—a toxic relationship she once escaped.

Because she was spiritually disconnected, she was emotionally vulnerable. She gave in, telling herself it was just for comfort.

That's how temptation gains ground: when your spiritual life weakens, so does your resistance.

c) Missed Opportunities for Kingdom Impact - Missed opportunities for Kingdom impact refer to moments when a believer fails to act, speak, or serve in a way that advances God's will or reveals His love, often because of fear, distraction, disobedience, or lack of spiritual awareness.

It's when God opens a door to reach someone, show compassion, share truth, or serve—and we ignore it, delay it, or walk past it.

d) Stunted Spiritual Growth and Maturity - Stunted spiritual growth refers to a condition in which a believer fails to develop in faith, character, and understanding of God due to neglect, disobedience, spiritual laziness, or failure to respond to correction.

It is a lack of progress in becoming more Christ-like—remaining spiritually immature even after receiving the truth.

A young lady at the ministry started well, participated at the worship team has attended church every Sunday. She knows the songs, the routines, and can quote scripture. But when trials come, she responds with fear instead of faith. She rarely prays on her own, doesn't serve anymore, and easily takes offense and leaves the church.

Despite years in the church, her spiritual maturity is stuck. Why? Because she never applies the Word, seeks depth, or allows God to stretch her.

She looks "planted"—but there's no growth.

e) Risk of Backsliding or Falling Away- Backsliding or falling away refers to the gradual or deliberate turning away from one's faith, commitment to God, or spiritual practices. It often begins with neglecting prayer, scripture, or obedience and leads to a weakened relationship with God—sometimes resulting in open sin, doubt, or abandonment of faith altogether.

The risk of backsliding increases when a person becomes spiritually complacent, disconnected from fellowship, or overwhelmed by worldly influences.

A husband was once active in church, prayer, and Bible study. But after a season of disappointment and unanswered prayers, he stopped attending services. At first, he said he just needed "a break." Soon, he stopped praying altogether. Old habits crept in—bitterness, gossip, pornography.

He still believed in God but no longer walked with Him. His heart drifted, and without accountability or spiritual fuel, he slipped backward into a life that God had once delivered him from.

Self-Diagnostic Questions:

- When was the last time I felt genuinely excited about my faith?
- Do I look forward to spending time with God in prayer and His Word?
- How has my giving (time, talents, resources) to God's work changed recently?
- Am I more concerned with God's opinion or others' opinions?
- Do I regularly share my faith with others?
- How often do I think about spiritual matters throughout my day?

The Illusion of Life in a Lukewarm Church

A church that has great music, events, and programs—but rarely preaches repentance, avoids uncomfortable truths, and never encourages deep discipleship—might look alive, but could be spiritually lukewarm.

Its members may say they love God, but lack evidence of transformation, urgency, or surrender in daily life.

Impact on Corporate Worship and Ministry

When a church becomes lukewarm—spiritually indifferent, half-committed, or passionless, it deeply affects the atmosphere of worship and the effectiveness of ministry. What was meant to be a vibrant, Spirit-filled community becomes dry, routine, and powerless.

- Lukewarm worship lacks authenticity and hunger for God.
- Songs are sung, hands may be lifted, but hearts are far from God (Isaiah 29:13).
- The congregation may go through the motions, but there's no true encounter, no surrender, no transformation.

"These people honor me with their lips, but their hearts are far from me."
— *Matthew 15:8*

Effects on Church Growth and Community Impact

When a church's passion declines and it becomes spiritually lukewarm, the consequences extend far beyond Sunday services. The vitality, outreach, and influence of the church in its community and beyond suffer deeply.

Lukewarm churches struggle to attract new members. Visitors sense the lack of genuine enthusiasm, authentic worship, and vibrant community life. Without excitement or visible transformation, newcomers often feel uninspired to stay.

Existing members become disengaged or leave. Spiritual complacency leads to boredom, discouragement, or seeking more vibrant expressions of faith elsewhere.

The church's growth stagnates or declines, resulting in fewer leaders, volunteers, and resources over time.

The church is called to be salt and light in the world (Matthew 5:13-16)—a transformative presence in every sphere of life. When the church becomes lukewarm, it loses the very essence that enables it to fulfill this mission.

Historical Examples of Spiritual Renewal

Brief overview of revivals that addressed widespread spiritual lukewarmness:

a) The Great Awakening- The Great Awakening was a powerful spiritual revival movement that swept through the American colonies during the 18th century, roughly between the 1730s and 1770s. It was marked by renewed religious fervor, widespread evangelical preaching, and a deep emphasis on personal faith and repentance.

Key features include:

- Emphasis on Personal Conversion: People were urged to experience a personal, heartfelt relationship with God rather than relying solely on formal church rituals.
- Revival Meetings: Large outdoor gatherings and passionate sermons stirred many to repentance and spiritual renewal.
- Impact on Society: The movement challenged established religious authorities, encouraged individual religious freedom, and contributed to the growth of new denominations like Methodists and Baptists.
- Social and Political Effects: It helped foster ideas of equality and liberty that influenced the American Revolution and shaped early American culture.

b) The Welsh Revival - The Welsh Revival was a significant Christian revival movement that took place in Wales between 1904 and 1905. It sparked a widespread renewal of faith, leading to thousands of conversions and profound changes in communities across the country.

Key points include:

- Origins: The revival began with prayer meetings and passionate

preaching led by figures such as Evan Roberts.
- Spiritual Impact: The revival emphasized repentance, holiness, and a deep sense of the Holy Spirit's presence.
- Social Changes: It led to reduced crime rates, closure of pubs, and stronger family and church life as many people turned away from sin.
- Global Influence: The Welsh Revival inspired other revival movements worldwide and is remembered as a powerful example of spiritual awakening.

c) The Azusa Street Revival- The Azusa Street Revival was a historic Pentecostal revival that began in 1906 in Los Angeles, California, led by William J. Seymour, an African-American preacher. It is widely regarded as the birth of the modern Pentecostal movement.

Key Highlights:

- Spiritual Outpouring: The revival was marked by powerful experiences of the Holy Spirit, including speaking in tongues, healing, and prophecy.
- Racial Integration: It was notable for its interracial gatherings during a time of racial segregation in America, with people of different races worshiping together.
- Global Impact: The revival sparked Pentecostalism worldwide, influencing millions and leading to the growth of numerous Pentecostal denominations.
- Emphasis on Holy Spirit: The movement emphasized baptism in the Holy Spirit as a distinct experience for believers, empowering them for ministry and holy living.

Hope for the Lukewarm

Being lukewarm is a warning, not a sentence. With genuine repentance and a desire to grow, every believer can find renewed hope and a restored, vibrant faith

Though Christ's warning to the Laodicean church (Revelation 3:14–22) is severe, His tone is not rejection but relentless love.

How to Move from Lukewarm to On Fire

A. Recognize Your State

- Laodicea thought they were "rich" but were spiritually bankrupt (Revelation 3:17).
- Ask God: *"Search me, Lord. Show me where I've grown cold."* (Psalm 139:23–24).

B. Respond to Christ's Knock

- Repentance isn't guilt; it's turning back to God's embrace.
- Action Step: *Identify one area of compromise (e.g., prayerlessness, secret sin, pride) and surrender it today.*

C. Rekindle Your First Love

- *"Remember the height from which you have fallen! Repent and do the things you did at first."* (Revelation 2:4–5).
- Practical Ways:
- Return to daily Scripture (Jeremiah 15:16).
- Restore authentic worship (John 4:23–24).
- Reconnect with fervent believers (Hebrews 10:24–25).

A Prayer for Renewal:

- *"Lord, I confess my lukewarm heart. Forgive me for settling for half-hearted faith. Ignite Your fire in me again. I open the door—come in and transform me. In Jesus' name, Amen."*

Conclusion: Recognizing spiritual lukewarmness is the first step towards rekindling the flame of passionate faith. As we diagnose our spiritual condition honestly, we open ourselves to the transformative work of the Holy Spirit. The Baptism of Fire offers a powerful antidote to lukewarmness, promising to ignite a renewed fervor and commitment in our walk with God.

In the next chapter, we'll explore practical steps to prepare our hearts for the Baptism of Fire, setting the stage for a profound encounter with God's renewing presence.

Chapter 4: Barriers to the Fire

"*But whoever drinks the water I give them will never thirst. Indeed, the water I give them will become in them a spring of water welling up to eternal life.*" — John 4:14

The flame of God burns eternally, yet so often we find ourselves cold, distant, and spiritually stagnant. Like the Israelites who built golden calves while Moses communed with the Almighty on Mount Sinai, we too construct barriers between ourselves and the consuming fire of God's presence. These obstacles, both seen and unseen, quench the Spirit's work in our lives and diminish the transformative power that should characterize every believer.

The Weight of Tradition

Perhaps no barrier stands taller than the fortress of dead tradition. Jesus Himself confronted this when He told the Pharisees, "You have let go of the commands of God and are holding on to human traditions" (Mark 7:8). In our modern churches, we often mistake familiarity for faithfulness, confusing the preservation of methods with the preservation of the message.

Consider Geraldine, a longtime church member who had served faithfully in our ministry for over six years. When new leadership proposed contemporary worship alongside traditional services, she felt personally attacked. "This isn't how we've always done things," she protested. Her resistance wasn't rooted in theological conviction but in the comfort of predictability. The familiar hymns, the established order of service, the same prayers recited each week, these had become her spiritual security blanket.

But God is not confined to our preferences. The fire of revival throughout history has consistently broken through traditional barriers. The Great Awakening didn't emerge from established religious structures but often in spite of them. When we grip our traditions so tightly that they become idols, we inadvertently build walls against the very Spirit we claim to serve.

This doesn't mean abandoning all traditions. Scripture itself is our foundational tradition. Rather, it means distinguishing between biblical tradition that strengthens faith and human tradition that constrains it. The apostle Paul demonstrated this balance when he wrote, "Stand firm and hold fast to the teachings we passed on to you" (2 Thessalonians 2:15), while simultaneously breaking cultural barriers to reach the Gentiles.

The Poison of Pride

Pride masquerades as many things in the church: theological superiority, denominational loyalty, spiritual elitism, and personal righteousness. It whispers lies that sound almost biblical: "We have the truth," "Our way is more scriptural," "We're more committed than those lukewarm believers." This spiritual pride creates barriers not only between denominations but between individual believers and their desperate need for God's grace.

The Pharisee in Jesus' parable thanked God that he was "not like other people—robbers, evildoers, adulterers—or even like this tax collector" (Luke 18:11). His pride blinded him to his own spiritual poverty while preventing him from experiencing the transformative mercy that the humble tax collector received. Similarly, when we position ourselves as spiritually superior, we create barriers that keep us from the very humility required for spiritual renewal.

Pride also manifests in our reluctance to acknowledge areas where we need growth. Churches split over secondary doctrines while major cities remain unreached. Denominations compete for members while communities cry out for hope. Individual believers argue over worship styles while their own prayer lives remain anemic. This pride-driven division grieves the Holy Spirit and extinguishes the fire that could transform both church and culture.

The antidote to pride is found in Paul's words: "Do nothing out of selfish ambition or vain conceit. Rather, in humility value others above yourselves" (Philippians 2:3). When we approach fellow believers with genuine humility, recognizing that we all stand in need of grace, the barriers begin to crumble, and the Spirit finds room to work.

The Wilderness of Comfort

Perhaps the subtlest barrier to spiritual fire is the seductive power of comfort. We live in an age of unprecedented ease, where even our sufferings pale in comparison to the persecution faced by believers throughout history. This comfort, while not inherently evil, can become a spiritual narcotic that lulls us into complacency.

The church in Laodicea exemplified this danger. "You say, 'I am rich; I have acquired wealth and do not need a thing,'" Jesus declared, "But you do not realize that you are wretched, pitiful, poor, blind and naked" (Revelation 3:17). Their material prosperity had created spiritual poverty. They had mistaken external success for internal vitality.

Modern believers often fall into the same trap. We attend comfortable services in comfortable buildings, surrounded by comfortable people who think comfortable thoughts. We've domesticated the gospel, reducing the radical call to discipleship to a weekly religious appointment. The fire of God burns hottest when we step outside our comfort zones, when we encounter our desperate need for divine intervention.

This comfort extends beyond material wealth to emotional and spiritual comfort zones. We prefer sermons that affirm rather than convict, prayers that soothe rather than challenge, and fellowship that entertains rather than transforms. Yet throughout Scripture, God's most powerful work occurred when His people found themselves in uncomfortable circumstances—the Israelites in slavery, the disciples in persecution, the early church scattered by opposition.

Breaking through the barrier of comfort requires intentional discomfort. It means engaging with difficult passages of Scripture that challenge our assumptions. It involves serving in ways that stretch our abilities and expose our inadequacies. It demands prayer that moves beyond requests for blessing to requests for brokenness—the kind of brokenness that creates space for God's power to be made perfect in our weakness.

The Fog of Unforgiveness

Nothing quenches spiritual fire more effectively than the bitter poison of unforgiveness. Like carbon monoxide, it's often invisible but always deadly. Churches harbor decades-old conflicts, believers nurse grudges against family members, and entire denominations maintain historical animosities that prevent the unity Christ prayed for in John 17.

The barrier of unforgiveness operates on multiple levels. Personal unforgiveness creates internal barriers that block our connection with God. Jesus was explicit: "If you do not forgive others their trespasses, neither will your Father forgive your trespasses" (Matthew 6:15). This isn't because God's forgiveness is conditional, but because unforgiveness creates a heart condition that cannot receive or experience the forgiveness already offered.

Corporate unforgiveness creates barriers between believers that undermine the church's witness. When denominations refuse to acknowledge past wrongs, when churches split over personalities rather than principles, when believers publicly attack one another over secondary issues, the watching world sees not the love of Christ but the pride of humanity. This division not only grieves the Spirit but also provides ammunition for those who would dismiss Christianity as merely another human institution.

The path through unforgiveness begins with recognizing its presence. Often, we've grown so accustomed to our resentments that we no longer notice their weight. Like a person carrying a heavy backpack who gradually adjusts to the burden, we accommodate unforgiveness until it becomes our normal state. The first step toward freedom is acknowledging the load we've been carrying.

Forgiveness doesn't require forgetting, minimizing the offense, or trusting the offender. Rather, it involves releasing our right to revenge and our demand for retribution. It means choosing to pray blessings over those who have hurt us, even when our emotions rebel against such prayers. This choice repeated daily if necessary, gradually dismantles the barriers that have blocked the Spirit's work in our lives.

The Distraction of Busyness

Modern church life often resembles a religious hamster wheel—constant motion producing minimal progress. We've confused activity with spirituality, mistaking busy schedules for faithful service. This barrier of busyness prevents the very stillness required for spiritual renewal.

Martha exemplified this barrier when she complained to Jesus about Mary's choice to sit at His feet rather than help with meal preparation. Jesus' gentle rebuke reveals the heart of the issue: "Martha, Martha, you are worried and upset about many things, but few things are needed—or indeed only one. Mary has chosen what is better, and it will not be taken away from her" (Luke 10:41-42).

CHAPTER 4: BARRIERS TO THE FIRE

Church calendars overflow with activities: committee meetings, social events, fundraisers, programs, and services. While many of these activities serve legitimate purposes, they can collectively create a barrier to the deep, transformative work of the Spirit. We become so busy doing things for God that we lose touch with God Himself.

This busyness barrier affects both individual believers and entire congregations. Personal devotional time gets squeezed out by church activities. Families find themselves rushing from one church event to another without time for meaningful spiritual conversation. Ministers become program administrators rather than shepherds, measuring success by attendance figures rather than spiritual transformation.

The antidote to busyness isn't inactivity but intentionality. It requires saying no to good things in order to make room for the best things. It means scheduling margin in our lives—spaces of time deliberately left unfilled where the Spirit can work. It involves regular evaluation of our commitments, asking not "Can we do this?" but "Should we do this?"

The Mirror of Self-Reliance

Perhaps no barrier is more American than self-reliance. Our culture celebrates independence, self-sufficiency, and personal achievement. These values, while useful in many contexts, become spiritual obstacles when they prevent us from acknowledging our desperate need for divine intervention.

The Israelites in the wilderness provide a powerful example of this barrier. When God provided manna, He specifically instructed them not to store it overnight (except before the Sabbath). Those who disobeyed found their hoarded manna filled with worms and stinking by morning (Exodus 16:20). God was teaching them daily dependence, but their natural inclination was toward self-sufficiency.

Modern believers often approach their spiritual lives with the same self-reliant attitude. We attend church when convenient, pray when desperate, and give when comfortable. We treat God like a divine vending machine—depositing good deeds and expecting blessings in return. This transactional approach to faith creates barriers that prevent the deep relationship God desires with His people.

Self-reliance also manifests in our problem-solving approaches. Rather than beginning with prayer, we begin with planning. Instead of seeking God's wisdom, we consult human experts. We exhaust our own resources before acknowledging our need for divine intervention. While God has given us minds using and responsibilities to fulfill, He desires to be our first resource, not our last resort.

Breaking through the barrier of self-reliance requires cultivating a spirit of dependence. This begins with acknowledging that "apart from me you can do nothing" (John 15:5) is not hyperbole but literal truth. It involves starting each day with surrender rather than planning, asking "What do You want to do through me today?" rather than "What can I accomplish today?"

The Bridge of Brokenness

These barriers—tradition, pride, comfort, unforgiveness, busyness, and self-reliance—share a common solution: brokenness. Not the destructive brokenness of sin, but the redemptive brokenness that acknowledges our limitations and creates space for God's unlimited power.

The prophet Joel proclaimed, "Rend your heart and not your garments. Return to the Lord your God, for he is gracious and compassionate, slow to anger and abounding in love" (Joel 2:13). This heart-rending involves more than emotional response; it requires dismantling the barriers we've constructed between ourselves and God's consuming fire.

Brokenness begins with honest assessment. Like , we must pray, "Search me, God, and know my heart; test me and know my anxious thoughts. See if there is any offensive way in me and lead me in the way everlasting" (Psalm 139:23-24). This prayer invites divine examination of our barriers, trusting that God's revelation leads to liberation.

True brokenness also involves corporate acknowledgment. Churches must honestly assess their barriers, confessing where traditions have become idols, where pride has created division, where comfort has bred complacency. This corporate confession creates an atmosphere where the Spirit can move freely, bringing renewal that transforms both individual believers and entire congregations.

The Promise Beyond the Barriers

God's promise remains unchanged: "If my people, who are called by my name, will humble themselves and pray and seek my face and turn from their wicked ways, then I will hear from heaven, and I will forgive their sin and will heal their land" (2 Chronicles 7:14). The pathway to spiritual renewal runs directly through the demolition of the barriers we've constructed.

When these obstacles are removed, the fire of God finds fresh fuel. Hearts long cold begin to burn with renewed passion. Churches experience genuine revival rather than manufactured excitement. Communities witness transformation that can only be explained by divine intervention.

The barriers to the fire are real, but they are not permanent. Like the walls of Jericho, they can fall when God's people approach them in His prescribed manner. The question remains: Are we willing to identify and demolish the barriers in our own lives and churches? Are we prepared for the consuming fire that awaits on the other side?

The flame of God burns eternally, waiting for hearts and churches brave enough to remove the barriers that have kept it at bay. The choice is ours, and the time is now.

Chapter 5: The Process of Rekindling

The embers still glow beneath the ashes of routine. Though the barriers have dimmed our spiritual fire, they have not extinguished it entirely. Deep within every believer burns the indestructible flame of God's Spirit—sometimes barely visible, often covered by the debris of disappointment and distraction, but never fully quenched. The process of rekindling this fire is both divine mystery and practical reality, requiring both God's sovereign work and our intentional participation.

"For this reason I remind you to fan into flame the gift of God, which is in you through the laying on of my hands. For the Spirit God gave us does not make us timid, but gives us power, love and self-discipline." — 2 Timothy 1:6-7

Like a skilled craftsman coaxing life from dying coals, the Holy Spirit waits to breathe fresh fire into hearts prepared to receive it. But rekindling is not a single moment; it is a process—sometimes gentle, sometimes dramatic, always transformative. Understanding this process equips us to cooperate with the Spirit's work rather than resist it, to fan the flames rather than smother them.

The Preparation of the Heart

Before any fire can be rekindled, the heart must be prepared. In the spiritual realm, this preparation begins with what the Puritans called

CHAPTER 5: THE PROCESS OF REKINDLING

"the preparation of the heart"—a deliberate positioning of our souls to receive fresh fire from heaven. This preparation is not merely human effort but a divine-human cooperation where God prepares hearts that willingly submit to His preparation.

King Josiah exemplified this heart preparation during Judah's spiritual renewal. "Neither before nor after Josiah was there a king like him who turned to the Lord as he did—with all his heart and with all his soul and with all his strength, in accordance with all the Law of Moses" (2 Kings 23:25). His wholehearted turning preceded and enabled the sweeping reforms that followed.

Heart preparation begins with honest assessment. Like a homeowner examining a house before renovation, we must courageously evaluate the current state of our spiritual lives. This requires asking difficult questions: When did I last experience genuine spiritual hunger? What areas of my life remain untouched by Christ's lordship? Where have I settled for religious routine instead of a relationship?

This assessment must be bathed in grace, not condemnation. The purpose is not self-flagellation but recognition—acknowledging where we are so we can understand where God wants to take us. The prodigal son's return began when he "came to his senses" (Luke 15:17), recognizing his true condition without descending into hopeless despair.

Heart preparation also involves clearing away accumulated debris. Just as a fireplace must be cleaned of old ashes before new logs can burn effectively, our hearts must be cleared of spiritual clutter that inhibits fresh fire. This includes confessing known sin, releasing long-held grudges, surrendering cherished idols, and abandoning self-sufficient attitudes that have hindered intimacy with God.

The prophet Hosea captured this preparation: "Sow righteousness for yourselves, reap the fruit of unfailing love, and break up your unplowed ground; for it is time to seek the Lord, until he comes and showers his righteousness on you" (Hosea 10:12). Breaking up unplowed ground is hard work, but it creates soil where the seeds of revival can take root and flourish.

The Discipline of Seeking

Rekindling spiritual fire requires more than passive waiting; it demands active seeking. The Hebrew word "darash," often translated as "seek," carries the connotation of persistent pursuit, like a detective following clues or a lover pursuing the beloved. This seeking is not occasional but habitual, not casual but desperate.

Jeremiah proclaimed God's promise: "You will seek me and find me when you seek me with all your heart" (Jeremiah 29:13). This wholehearted seeking distinguishes genuine spiritual hunger from religious performance. It moves beyond asking God to bless our plans to desperately wanting God's presence regardless of the cost.

Daniel exemplified this discipline of seeking during Israel's captivity. "So, I turned to the Lord God and pleaded with him in prayer and petition, in fasting, and in sackcloth and ashes" (Daniel 9:3). His seeking involved multiple dimensions: prayer, fasting, and physical expressions of spiritual desperation. This multi-faceted approach created an environment where God could reveal His purposes and power.

The discipline of seeking manifests differently for each believer, but certain elements appear consistently across Scripture and church history. Extended prayer—moving beyond brief requests to prolonged communion—forms the foundation of seeking. This includes both individual prayer and corporate prayer, both spoken petitions and listening silence.

Fasting often accompanies genuine seeking, not as a manipulative tool to gain God's attention but as a physical expression of spiritual priority. When we voluntarily abstain from legitimate pleasures to focus on God, we declare that our hunger for Him supersedes our other appetites. This declaration, lived out practically, creates space for the Spirit to work in ways that our constant consumption would otherwise prevent.

Scripture meditation provides fuel for the seeking heart. Unlike casual Bible reading, meditation involves slowly chewing on God's Word until its nutrients penetrate our spiritual bloodstream. The psalmist described this process: "But whose delight is in the law of the Lord, and who meditates on his Law Day and night" (Psalm 1:2). This consistent engagement with Scripture creates a mind increasingly aligned with God's thoughts and a heart increasingly receptive to His fire.

The Dynamics of Surrender

At the heart of the rekindling process lies surrender—the voluntary relinquishment of control that creates space for God's sovereign work. This surrender is neither passive resignation nor self-destruction but active cooperation with divine purposes. It echoes Mary's response to the angel: "I am the Lord's servant. May your word to me be fulfilled" (Luke 1:38).

Surrender begins with acknowledging God's ownership of our lives. We are not our own; we have been bought with a price (1 Corinthians 6:19-20). This acknowledgment moves beyond intellectual agreement to practical implications. If God owns us, then He has the right to direct our careers, relationships, resources, and dreams according to His purposes rather than our preferences.

This surrender often involves releasing specific outcomes we've demanded from God. Abraham exemplified this when he raised the knife over Isaac, surrendering his promised future to God's inscrutable will (Genesis 22:10). His willingness to sacrifice what he loved most demonstrated the complete surrender that makes space for God's miraculous intervention.

Modern believers face similar surrender challenges. The successful executive must surrender career ambitions that conflict with family calling. The gifted minister must surrender ego needs that prevent collaboration with other leaders. The committed parent must surrender protective instincts that would shelter children from God's call to dangerous service. Each surrender creates space for God's fire to burn more brightly.

Surrender also involves embracing vulnerability. We naturally protect ourselves from disappointment, criticism, and failure. But spiritual fire burns brightly in vulnerable hearts that risk being hurt rather than remaining safe. This vulnerability allows others to see our struggles, weaknesses, and failures—transparency that creates authentic community and demonstrates the reality of God's grace in imperfect people.

The paradox of surrender is that it leads to true freedom. When we stop fighting God's purposes, we discover that His will aligns with our deepest longings. The restrictions we feared become protection, and the sacrifices we dreaded become doorways to greater joy than we could have imagined.

The Patience of Process

Rekindling spiritual fire rarely happens instantly. Like physical fire that begins with sparks, grows through kindling, and eventually produces roaring flames, spiritual rekindling follows a similar progression. Understanding this process prevents discouragement when immediate dramatic results don't appear and helps us cooperate with each stage of the Spirit's work.

The initial stage often involves subtle stirring—a growing dissatisfaction with spiritual status quo, an increasing hunger for authentic relationship with God, or a quiet conviction that more must be available than what we're currently experiencing. These stirrings may seem insignificant, but they signal the Spirit's preparatory work in our hearts.

Habakkuk experienced this stirring when he cried, "How long, Lord, must I call for help, but you do not listen?" (Habakkuk 1:2). His complaint revealed spiritual dissatisfaction that eventually led to deeper

CHAPTER 5: THE PROCESS OF REKINDLING

understanding of God's character and purposes. Similarly, our initial stirrings may manifest as spiritual frustration, but this frustration can become the starting point for renewed seeking.

The second stage typically involves increased spiritual activity—more consistent prayer, deeper Scripture study, greater involvement in Christian community, or renewed commitment to service. This activity is both response to the Spirit's stirring and preparation for greater work ahead. Like blowing on glowing coals, our spiritual disciplines provide oxygen that helps kindle the fire the Spirit is building.

During this stage, believers often experience both encouragement and confusion. Moments of clear divine presence alternate with periods of apparent silence. Old habits resist change while new spiritual appetites emerge. This tension is normal and necessary, reflecting the reality that transformation is a process rather than event.

The third stage brings more visible evidence of rekindling—changed priorities, increased spiritual sensitivity, bolder witness, deeper compassion, and genuine joy that doesn't depend on circumstances. Others begin noticing differences in our character, relationships, and responses to challenges. The fire that has been building internally begins expressing itself externally.

Throughout this process, patience remains essential. waited years between his anointing and his coronation. Joseph endured decades between his dreams and their fulfillment. Paul spent three years in Arabia after his Damascus Road encounter before beginning his missionary journeys. God's timing differs from our urgency, but His timing is always perfect.

This patience doesn't mean passivity. Rather, it involves continuing faithful spiritual disciplines while trusting God's sovereignty over results. We can control our seeking but not God's responding. We can prepare the hearth but not ignite the flame. We can clear away barriers but not manufacture breakthroughs. This balance between human responsibility and divine sovereignty characterizes the entire rekindling process.

The Maintenance of Flame

Rekindling is not a one-time event but an ongoing process requiring consistent maintenance. Like physical fire that dies without fuel and oxygen, spiritual fire requires regular attention and feeding. The disciplines that initiated rekindling must continue to sustain it, though they may evolve as our relationship with God deepens.

Regular Scripture engagement remains foundational. However, this engagement may shift from intensive study to contemplative meditation, from systematic reading to devotional reflection. The key is maintaining consistent contact with God's Word in whatever form most effectively feeds the flame.

Prayer continues as the primary means of maintaining intimacy with God. Rekindled believers often find their prayer lives becoming more conversational and less formal, more focused on relationship than requests. Many discover the value of silence in prayer, learning to listen as well as speak.

Community involvement becomes increasingly important as rekindled believers recognize their need for others and their responsibility to encourage fellow believers. However, this involvement focuses more on authentic relationships than religious activity, more on mutual encouragement than program participation.

Service provides an essential outlet for the love that rekindling produces. Without expression, even genuine spiritual fire can become self-focused and eventually diminish. Rekindled believers must find ways to pour out the life they've received, whether through formal ministry roles or informal acts of love and service.

Perhaps most importantly, maintaining spiritual fire requires protecting it from influences that would diminish or extinguish it. This involves wise choices about entertainment, relationships, priorities, and commitments. Not all influences are inherently evil, but some prove detrimental to spiritual vitality. Rekindled believers learn to evaluate decisions based on their impact on spiritual health rather than merely personal preference or social acceptability.

The Domino Effect

Authentic spiritual rekindling never remains private. Like a stone thrown into still water, it creates Dominos that extend far beyond the initial point of impact. Families, churches, communities, and even nations can be transformed when God's fire spreads from heart to heart through the mysterious but undeniable process of spiritual contagion.

The Great Awakening demonstrates this Domino effect on a massive scale. What began with individual believers experiencing spiritual renewal eventually transformed entire communities, influenced political movements, and shaped cultural values for generations.

This Domino effect operates through relationships. Rekindled spouses influence marriage partners, rekindled parents impact children, rekindled employees affect workplace atmosphere, and rekindled church members encourage fellow believers. The influence spreads not through preaching or persuasion but through the authentic demonstration of transformed life.

Understanding this Domino effect motivates perseverance during the rekindling process. Our personal spiritual condition affects not only our own relationship with God but also our influence on everyone around us. Conversely, our spiritual stagnation contributes to the cooling of others' spiritual temperature. We are never merely private believers but always members of an interconnected body where individual health affects corporate vitality.

The process of rekindling, therefore, carries both personal and corporate significance. As we submit to the Spirit's work in our own hearts, we participate in God's larger purposes for His church and His world. The flame He kindles in us is destined to spread, illuminating darkness wherever it goes and setting other hearts ablaze with the fire of His love.

The process continues, and the invitation remains open. Will we position ourselves to receive fresh fire? Will we persist through the stages of seeking, surrendering, and waiting? Will we maintain the flame once it's rekindled? The choice is ours, but the power is His. And He waits, even now, to breathe fresh fire into hearts prepared to burn for His glory.

Chapter 6: Walking in the Fire - Daily Spiritual Disciplines

The baptism of fire isn't a one-time event; it's an ongoing process. It's about living a life continually fueled by the Holy Spirit, allowing His fire to purify, empower, and guide us daily. This chapter explores essential spiritual disciplines that cultivate this ongoing fire within us, transforming us from passive observers into active participants in God's work.

I. **Fuel: Consistent Prayer**

- More Than a Request List: Prayer isn't just reciting a list of needs; it's intimate communion with God, a conversation that shapes our hearts and aligns our wills with His.
- Finding Your Prayer Rhythm: Experiment with different prayer styles (e.g., contemplative prayer, intercessory prayer, praying the Scriptures) to discover what resonates most deeply with you. Set aside dedicated time each day, even if it's just for 15 minutes.
- Praying Without Ceasing (1 Thessalonians 5:17): Integrate prayer into your daily activities. Turn mundane tasks into opportunities for conversation with God. Pray for those you encounter, for wisdom in decisions, and for strength in challenges.
- Journaling: Writing down your prayers, reflections, and insights

can deepen your understanding of God's leading and track His faithfulness over time.

II. Kindling the Flame: Immersing in the Word

- Beyond Information: Transformation: The Bible isn't just a collection of stories; it's the living Word of God, capable of transforming our hearts and minds.
- Intentional Study: Don't just read Scripture; study it. Use commentaries, concordances, and study Bibles to gain deeper understanding.
- Meditative Reading: Dwell on a single verse or passage, asking God to reveal its meaning and application to your life.
- Memorization: Hiding God's Word in your heart through memorization allows you to draw upon it in moments of temptation, doubt, or need.
- Application: The goal is not just to know Scripture, but to live it. Ask yourself, "How does this passage challenge me to change my thoughts, words, or actions?"

III. Stoking the Embers: Fellowship and Accountability

- The Body of Christ: Not a Solo Act: We are designed for community. Isolation extinguishes the fire; fellowship fans it into flame. Participate in a House of Prayer.
- Finding Your Tribe: Seek out a small group, Bible study, or accountability partner who will encourage you, challenge you, and pray for you.
- Authenticity and Vulnerability: Create a safe space where you can be honest about your struggles and receive support without judgment.
- Serving Together: Working alongside other believers in ministry ignites passion and strengthens the bonds of fellowship.

- Accountability: Invite trusted friends to hold you accountable in areas where you struggle, such as temptation, time management, or unhealthy habits.

IV. Removing the Ashes: Confession and Repentance

- Unconfessed Sin: A Fire Extinguisher: Sin smothers the spiritual fire, hindering our relationship with God and hindering our effectiveness.
- Regular Confession: Make confession a regular part of your prayer life, acknowledging your sins and asking for forgiveness.
- Turning Away (Repentance): Repentance is more than just saying "I'm sorry"; it's a conscious decision to turn away from sin and pursue righteousness.
- Seeking Forgiveness from Others: When we have wronged someone, we must seek their forgiveness, making amends whenever possible.
- Grace and Mercy: Remember that God's grace is always available to us, even when we stumble. Don't let guilt and shame keep you from seeking His forgiveness.

V. Spreading the Flame: Witness and Service

- Living Epistles: Our lives are a testimony to the power of God. Let your actions speak louder than your words.
- Sharing Your Story: Be prepared to share your personal story of how God has transformed your life.
- Serving Others: Look for opportunities to serve others in your community, your church, and your workplace.
- The Great Commission (Matthew 28:19-20): Be mindful of Jesus' command to go and make disciples of all nations.
- Love in Action: Demonstrate God's love through acts of kindness, compassion, and generosity.

Walking in the fire is a daily commitment to cultivating a vibrant relationship with God through consistent spiritual disciplines. It's about intentionally fueling the flame within us, allowing the Holy Spirit to transform us into vessels of His love, power, and grace. As we embrace these disciplines, we will experience a deeper intimacy with God, a greater sense of purpose, and a burning desire to share His love with the world. The fire will not only burn within us, but it will also spread to those around us, igniting a spiritual awakening in the Body of Christ.

Chapter 7: Maintaining the Fire Through Trials

The Christian life is not a guarantee of smooth sailing. In fact, Jesus warned us that we would face trials and tribulations (John 16:33). The true test of our faith is not whether we experience hardship, but how we respond to it. This chapter explores how to maintain the fire of the Holy Spirit burning brightly within us, even in the midst of life's most challenging seasons. Trials are inevitable, but spiritual defeat is not.

I. Understanding the Purpose of Trials

- More Than Just Punishment: While trials can sometimes be the consequence of our own actions, more often they are opportunities for growth, refinement, and deeper dependence on God.
- Testing and Refinement (1 Peter 1:6-7): Like gold refined by fire, our faith is purified and strengthened through trials. They reveal our weaknesses and vulnerabilities, prompting us to rely more fully on God's grace.
- Developing Perseverance (Romans 5:3-5): Trials cultivate perseverance, character, and hope. They teach us to endure hardship and to trust that God will see us through.
- Witness to Others: How we respond to trials can be a powerful

testimony to the world. When we demonstrate faith, peace, and joy in the midst of suffering, we point others to the hope that is found in Christ.
- God's Sovereignty: Even in the midst of trials, remember that God is in control. He has a purpose for everything that happens in our lives, even if we don't understand it at the time.

II. **Strategies for Maintaining the Fire**

- Cling to God's Promises:
- Remember His Faithfulness: Recall past instances where God has proven faithful in your life. Dwell on His promises in Scripture, and declare them over your situation.
- Specific Promises for Trials: Identify specific verses that offer comfort, strength, and hope in times of trouble (e.g., Romans 8:28, Isaiah 41:10, Psalm 23:4).
- Intensify Prayer and Scripture Study:
- Run to God, Not Away: Trials often tempt us to withdraw from God, but this is precisely the time when we need Him most. Pour out your heart to Him in prayer, seeking His guidance and comfort.
- Find Strength in the Word: Immerse yourself in Scripture, allowing God's Word to renew your mind and strengthen your spirit. Look for passages that address your specific struggles.
- Lean on the Body of Christ:
- Don't Isolate Yourself: Resist the urge to withdraw from the community. Surround yourself with supportive friends and family who can offer encouragement, prayer, and practical assistance.
- Be Vulnerable and Honest: Share your struggles with trusted confidants. Allow them to minister to you and to remind you of God's love.
- Receive Prayer and Encouragement: Allow others to pray for you

and to speak words of hope and encouragement into your life.
- Practice Gratitude:
- Focus on the Blessings: Even in the midst of hardship, there are always things to be grateful for. Make a conscious effort to identify and appreciate the blessings in your life.
- Gratitude Journal: Keep a gratitude journal, writing down the things you are thankful for each day. This can help shift your focus from your problems to God's provision.
- Renew Your Mind:
- Guard Your Thoughts: Trials can often lead to negative thinking patterns. Be intentional about replacing negative thoughts with positive, faith-filled thoughts.
- Confess Truth: Speak God's truth over your situation, even when you don't feel like it. Declare His promises and affirm His sovereignty.
- Limit Exposure to Negativity: Minimize your exposure to negative news, social media, and toxic relationships.

III. **Common Pitfalls to Avoid**

- Bitterness and Resentment: These emotions will extinguish the fire of the Spirit. Forgive those who have wronged you and release any bitterness you may be holding onto.
- Self-Pity: Dwelling on your own suffering will only deepen your despair. Focus on serving others and on the needs of those around you.
- Doubt and Unbelief: Trials can challenge our faith, but we must resist the temptation to doubt God's goodness and faithfulness. Cling to His promises and trust that He is working all things together for our good.
- Spiritual Neglect: Don't neglect your spiritual disciplines during times of trial. Continue to pray, read Scripture, and fellowship with

other believers.
- Making Hasty Decisions: Avoid making major life decisions in the midst of a trial. Seek wise counsel and wait for God's clear direction.

IV. **Emerging Stronger**

- Deeper Dependence on God: Trials can lead us to a deeper understanding of our own limitations and a greater reliance on God's strength.
- Increased Compassion for Others: Having experienced suffering ourselves, we are better equipped to empathize with and minister to others who are going through difficult times.
- Greater Spiritual Maturity: Trials have the potential to produce greater spiritual maturity and Christ-likeness in our lives.
- A More Powerful Testimony: Our stories of overcoming adversity can inspire others to persevere in their own trials.

Maintaining the fire through trials is not easy, but it is possible. By understanding the purpose of trials, employing effective strategies, avoiding common pitfalls, and embracing God's grace, we can emerge from the fires of adversity stronger, more resilient, and more radiant than ever before. The fire of the Holy Spirit, far from being extinguished, can burn even brighter, illuminating the path for others and glorifying God in the midst of our suffering.

Chapter 8: The Fire's Purpose - Mission and Ministry

The baptism of fire is not just a personal experience; it's a commissioning. The Holy Spirit doesn't ignite us for our own enjoyment, but to propel us into action, to equip us to be witnesses and agents of transformation in the world. This chapter delves into how the fire of the Spirit fuels our mission and ministry, empowering us to extend God's Kingdom and impact lives for eternity.

I. Understanding God's Mission (Missio Dei)

- More Than Just Evangelism: While sharing the Gospel is a vital part of God's mission, it's not the whole picture. God's mission encompasses the restoration of all things – spiritual, social, economic, and environmental.
- The Kingdom of God: Jesus proclaimed the Kingdom of God, a reality of God's reign and rule being established on earth as it is in heaven. We are called to participate in extending this Kingdom through our words and actions.
- Love in Action: God's mission is rooted in love – love for God and love for our neighbor. We demonstrate this love by meeting the needs of others, advocating for justice, and working for the common good.

- A Holistic Approach: God's mission addresses the whole person – body, soul, and spirit. We are called to minister to people's physical, emotional, and spiritual needs.
- The Great Commission (Matthew 28:19-20) and the Great Commandment (Matthew 22:37-40): These two mandates summarize God's mission for His people: to make disciples and to love God and our neighbor.

II. **The Fire's Empowerment for Ministry**

- Gifts of the Spirit (1 Corinthians 12): The Holy Spirit equips us with spiritual gifts to fulfill specific roles in ministry. These gifts are not for our own benefit, but for the building up of the Body of Christ and the advancement of God's Kingdom.
- Passion and Purpose: The fire of the Spirit ignites a passion within us for a particular area of ministry. This passion fuels our dedication and perseverance, enabling us to overcome obstacles and make a lasting impact.
- Courage and Boldness: The Holy Spirit empowers us to speak the truth with boldness, even in the face of opposition. He gives us the courage to step out of our comfort zones and to take risks for the sake of the Gospel.
- Compassion and Empathy: The fire of the Spirit softens our hearts and enables us to empathize with the suffering of others. This compassion motivates us to act on their behalf and to bring healing and restoration.
- Supernatural Power: The Holy Spirit empowers us to perform miracles, heal the sick, and cast out demons. This supernatural power confirms the truth of the Gospel and demonstrates the reality of God's Kingdom.

III. Identifying Your Ministry Calling

- Prayerful Discernment: Seek God's guidance through prayer, asking Him to reveal your unique calling and purpose.
- Spiritual Gifts Assessment: Identify your spiritual gifts through testing and experimentation. Ask others to affirm your gifts and to provide feedback on your strengths and weaknesses.
- Passion and Interests: Consider your passions, interests, and experiences. What are you naturally drawn to? What problems do you want to solve?
- Needs in the Community: Look around you and identify the needs in your community, your church, and your workplace. Where can you make a difference?
- Mentorship and Guidance: Seek the counsel of mature Christians who can provide wisdom, encouragement, and accountability.

IV. Diverse Expressions of Ministry

- Beyond the Pulpit: Ministry is not limited to pastors and missionaries. Every believer is called to serve God in some capacity, whether it's through teaching, leading, serving, giving, or simply being a loving presence in the lives of others.
- Everyday Opportunities: Look for opportunities to minister in your everyday life, at home, at work, and in your community.
- Specific Areas of Ministry: Consider serving in areas such as:
- Evangelism: Sharing the Gospel with those who have not yet heard.
- Discipleship: Helping new believers grow in their faith.
- Mercy Ministries: Serving the poor, the homeless, and the marginalized.
- Teaching: Equipping others with biblical knowledge and practical skills.

- Leadership: Guiding and mentoring others.
- Creative Arts: Using your artistic talents to glorify God.
- Intercession: Praying for the needs of others.

Tabitha, a leader in our Ministry responsible for the community outreach program, wasn't afraid to admit she needed guidance. Despite her passion and experience, she recognized the weight of responsibility and the potential for burnout. Instead of relying solely on her own strength, Tabitha proactively sought mentorship from her mentor and church leaders.

Her accountability wasn't just a formality; it was woven into her leadership style. She openly shared her vision, challenges, and even her doubts with her mentors, creating a safe space for honest feedback. She actively sought their advice on strategic decisions, program implementation, and even her own personal well-being.

Tabitha wasn't afraid of critique. She embraced constructive criticism, using it to refine her approach and grow as a leader. She regularly asked for input from her team members, ensuring that diverse voices were heard and valued. She understood that true leadership wasn't about having all the answers but about fostering a collaborative and accountable environment.

Because of her commitment to accountability, Tabitha built a team that trusted her leadership and felt empowered to contribute their best in reaching out to the homeless. Her program thrived, not just because of her hard work, but because of the collective wisdom and shared responsibility she cultivated. Tabitha's example demonstrates that accountable leadership isn't a sign of weakness, but a hallmark of strength, wisdom, and a genuine commitment to serving others effectively.

V. **Sustaining a Life of Ministry**

- Prioritize Spiritual Disciplines: Continue to cultivate your relationship with God through prayer, Scripture study, and fellowship.
- Maintain Healthy Boundaries: Avoid burnout by setting healthy boundaries and taking time for rest and recreation.
- Seek Accountability: Surround yourself with trusted friends who can hold you accountable and provide encouragement.
- Embrace Lifelong Learning: Continue to grow in your knowledge and skills, seeking opportunities for training and development.
- Celebrate Successes: Take time to celebrate your accomplishments and to give thanks to God for His blessings.

The fire of the Holy Spirit is intended to ignite a passion for God's mission within us. By understanding God's heart for the world, embracing our spiritual gifts, and stepping out in faith, we can become powerful agents of transformation, extend His Kingdom and impacting lives for eternity. Let the fire burn brightly within you, propelling you into a life of purpose, service, and lasting significance. The world is waiting for the Church to rise up and fulfill its mission, empowered by the Holy Spirit.

Chapter 9: The Signs of a Fire-Baptized Life

"But you will receive power when the Holy Spirit comes on you; and you will be my witnesses in Jerusalem, and in all Judea and Samaria, and to the ends of the earth." - Acts 1:8

The baptism of fire produces unmistakable changes in a believer's life. These transformations are not merely theoretical or invisible—they manifest in practical, observable ways that affect every aspect of our existence. Just as physical fire produces heat, light, and energy, spiritual fire generates characteristics that mark a life completely surrendered to God's transforming power.

Understanding these signs serves multiple purposes: it helps us evaluate our own spiritual condition, provides goals to pursue in our spiritual journey, and enables us to recognize fire-baptized believers who can mentor and encourage us. These signs are not achievements to be proud of but evidences of God's grace working through surrendered lives.

When John the Baptist proclaimed that Jesus would baptize with the Holy Spirit and fire, he spoke of a transformation so profound that it would be unmistakable to all who witnessed it. The fire baptism is not merely an emotional experience or a theological concept—it is a spiritual reality that produces visible, tangible evidence in the life of the believer. Just as physical fire leaves unmistakable marks on everything it touches, the fire of God leaves distinct signs in those who have been truly baptized by its power.

The Fire of Purification

The most immediate sign of a fire-baptized life is an ongoing process of purification that goes far deeper than surface behavior modification. Those touched by God's fire experience a divine intolerance for sin that extends beyond external compliance to internal transformation. They find themselves naturally gravitating away from attitudes, entertainment, relationships, and activities that once seemed harmless but now feel spiritually suffocating.

This purification is not primarily driven by human effort or religious duty, but by the inner work of the Holy Spirit who creates a new sensitivity to anything that grieves God. The fire-baptized believer discovers that compromise becomes increasingly uncomfortable, not because of external pressure, but because their redeemed nature rebels against anything that contradicts the character of Christ within them.

The process is both gentle and thorough, like a refiner's fire that burns away impurities while preserving what is precious. It manifests in a growing hunger for holiness, an increasing intolerance for spiritual mediocrity, and a deepening desire to be conformed to the image of Christ in every area of life.

Consuming Passion for God's Presence

Perhaps the most distinctive mark of the fire-baptized life is an insatiable hunger for God's presence. While others may be satisfied with knowing about God, those touched by His fire must know God Himself. They are drawn to prayer not as a duty but as a desperate need, like a drowning person gasps for air.

This passion manifests in extended times of worship that feel too short, prayer meetings that energize rather than drain, and a constant awareness of God's nearness throughout ordinary activities. The fire-baptized believer finds themselves talking to God while driving, worshiping while working, and seeking His face in quiet moments that others might fill with entertainment or distraction.

Their relationship with Scripture moves beyond academic study to intimate encounter. They read the Bible not merely to gain information but to hear God's voice, and they find that familiar passages suddenly burst with fresh revelation and personal application. The Word becomes alive, active, and transformative in ways they never experienced before the fire touched their hearts.

Boldness in Witness and Ministry

Fire produces both light and heat, and the fire-baptized believer cannot help but radiate both. There is a supernatural boldness that emerges, not from human confidence but from the overwhelming reality of what God has done in their life. They speak of Christ not because they feel they should, but because they cannot remain silent about what they have seen and experienced.

This boldness often surprises even the believers themselves. Those who once trembled at the thought of sharing their faith find themselves naturally steering conversations toward spiritual matters. They discover that opportunities for ministry seem to multiply, and they possess a courage to step into situations that would have intimidated them before their fire baptism.

The boldness extends beyond evangelism to every area of Christian service. They volunteer for challenging assignments, speak up in situations where others remain silent, and demonstrate a willingness to take spiritual risks that reveal their confidence in God's faithfulness and power.

Supernatural Love and Compassion

The fire of God burns away the barriers that separate us from others and replaces them with a supernatural love that flows from the heart of God Himself. Fire-baptized believers find themselves loving people they once found difficult to tolerate, showing compassion to those they previously judged, and interceding for individuals who have hurt or offended them.

This love is not sentimental or merely emotional—it is the practical, sacrificial love of Christ that seeks the highest good of others regardless of personal cost. It manifests in increased generosity, heightened sensitivity to the needs of others, and a willingness to invest time and energy in relationships that offer no obvious personal benefit.

The compassion extends particularly to the lost and broken. Fire-baptized believers develop God's heart for those trapped in sin, addiction, despair, and spiritual darkness. They see people not as inconveniences or projects but as eternal souls for whom Christ died, and they are willing to go to great lengths to see others experience the same transformation they have received.

Heightened Spiritual Discernment

The fire of God burns away spiritual dullness and replaces it with sharp discernment that operates beyond natural understanding. Fire-baptized believers develop an increased sensitivity to spiritual atmospheres, an ability to recognize the difference between flesh and spirit in ministry situations, and a supernatural insight into the deeper issues affecting people's lives.

This discernment helps them navigate relationships with wisdom, make decisions with confidence, and minister with effectiveness. They can sense when someone is struggling spiritually before it becomes obvious to others, recognize counterfeit spiritual activity, and discern God's direction in situations where others see only confusion.

The heightened discernment also produces a deep appreciation for authentic spiritual activity and an uncomfortable awareness of religious performance. They can distinguish between human effort and divine empowerment, between emotional manipulation and genuine spiritual breakthrough, and between programs that look successful and ministries that actually bear spiritual fruit.

Increased Fruitfulness in Kingdom Work

Just as natural fire accelerates chemical reactions and increases productivity, the fire of God dramatically increases spiritual fruitfulness in the life of the believer. Their prayers carry more authority, their witness produces more conversions, their service creates more lasting impact, and their leadership generates more genuine transformation in others.

This fruitfulness is not the result of human striving but of divine empowerment. Fire-baptized believers often find themselves accomplishing more with less effort because they are working in partnership with the Holy Spirit rather than relying solely on their own abilities. They experience supernatural favor, divine appointments, and miraculous provision that accelerate their effectiveness in Kingdom work.

The fruitfulness extends to every area of life—their families are blessed, their workplaces are influenced, their communities are impacted, and their churches are strengthened by their presence and participation.

Joy in the Midst of Trials

The fire of God produces a joy that is independent of circumstances and unshakeable in the face of opposition. Fire-baptized believers discover a supernatural ability to rejoice in trials, maintain peace in chaos, and express gratitude in difficult seasons. This is not mere positive thinking or emotional denial—it is the deep, settled joy that comes from knowing God is in control and working all things together for good.

This joy becomes a powerful witness to others who cannot understand how someone can maintain such peace and contentment while facing the same challenges that overwhelm them. It demonstrates the reality of God's presence and power in ways that argument and explanation cannot achieve.

The Call to Examination

These signs are not achievements to be attained through human effort but evidences of divine work that flows from genuine fire baptism. They serve as both encouragement for those who recognize them in their own lives and as an invitation for those who long to experience this deeper dimension of Christian living.

The question each believer must ask is not whether they can manufacture these signs through determination and discipline, but whether they are willing to position themselves for the fire of God to fall upon their lives. Are we hungry enough to seek it, humble enough to receive it, and surrendered enough to let it burn away everything that is not of God?

The fire is available. The signs are unmistakable. The choice is ours.

Chapter 10: Igniting Others - Passing the Flame

"And the things you have heard me say in the presence of many witnesses entrust to reliable people who will also be qualified to teach others." - 2 Timothy 2:2

The flickering candle that sits alone in a vast cathedral may provide enough light for one person to read, but it can never illuminate the entire sanctuary. However, when that single flame is used to light another candle, and that one lights another, soon the entire cathedral blazes with radiant light that drives away every shadow. This is the divine mathematics of spiritual multiplication—one flame becoming many, many becoming multitudes, until the darkness has no choice but to flee.

The rekindled spiritual flame in your own heart is never meant to remain a private blessing. It is a sacred trust, a holy fire that carries within it the responsibility and privilege of igniting others. The very nature of authentic spiritual renewal demands expression, multiplication, and expansion. A flame that does not spread will eventually die, but a flame that is intentionally shared becomes an unstoppable force for transformation.

The Mandate of Multiplication

Jesus never called His disciples to simply experience transformation—He called them to become transformers. The Great Commission is not merely about making converts; it is about making disciples who make disciples. This divine principle of spiritual multiplication runs like a golden thread through every great movement of God in history.

When John Wesley experienced his heart being "strangely warmed" at Aldersgate, he did not retreat into private mysticism. Instead, he spent the rest of his life igniting others with the same flame that had transformed his own soul. The Methodist revival that followed was not the work of one man, but of thousands of ordinary believers who caught the fire and passed it on to others. Class meetings, band societies, and field preaching all became vehicles for spiritual multiplication that eventually transformed entire nations.

The apostle Paul understood this principle intimately. His ministry strategy was never about building a personal empire or drawing crowds to hear his eloquent preaching. Instead, he focused on identifying, developing, and deploying spiritual sons and daughters who would carry the flame to places he could never reach. Timothy, Titus, Silas, Luke, Barnabas, and countless unnamed believers became living torches who carried the Gospel flame across the Roman Empire.

This same pattern must characterize our approach to spiritual renewal today. The flame that God has kindled in your heart through prayer, worship, Scripture, and surrender is not the end goal—it is the beginning of a divine chain reaction that has the potential to impact generations.

The Heart of a Flame-Bearer

CHAPTER 10: IGNITING OTHERS - PASSING THE FLAME

Before we can effectively ignite others, we must understand what it means to carry the flame with intentionality and wisdom. Not everyone who has experienced spiritual renewal automatically becomes effective at passing that flame to others. There are specific heart attitudes and character qualities that distinguish those who merely possess the flame from those who successfully multiply it.

A Burden for Others

The flame-bearer carries a holy discontent with the spiritual condition of those around them. This is not a critical or judgmental spirit, but rather a broken-hearted compassion that sees the potential for transformation in every person they encounter. They cannot rest easy knowing that others are living in spiritual darkness when the light of Christ could illuminate their path.

This burden manifests itself in various ways. Some are called to weep in intercession for the lost and lukewarm. Others feel compelled to speak boldly about the reality of spiritual renewal. Still others demonstrate their burden through acts of service and love that create opportunities for spiritual conversations. Regardless of the expression, the burden for others becomes the driving force that motivates consistent action.

A Servant's Heart

True flame-bearers understand that their role is not to be spiritual celebrities or to build their own reputation. Instead, they embrace the servant's heart that seeks to see others succeed and grow beyond their own level of spiritual maturity. They rejoice when their spiritual children surpass them in faith, gifting, and effectiveness.

This servant's heart expresses itself through patience with those who are slower to catch the flame, encouragement for those who struggle with doubt or discouragement, and wisdom in knowing when to speak and when to remain silent. The servant-hearted flame-bearer creates space for others to encounter God directly rather than becoming dependent on human mediators.

Authentic Transparency

Nothing kills the potential for spiritual multiplication faster than religious pretense or spiritual pride. People are not ignited by perfection—they are ignited by authenticity. The most effective flame-bearers are those who are honest about their own struggles, failures, and ongoing need for God's grace while simultaneously testifying to the transforming power of that grace.

This transparency creates an environment where others feel safe to be honest about their own spiritual condition. When people see that spiritual giants also wrestle with doubt, face temptation, and require constant dependence on God's strength, they realize that spiritual renewal is accessible to them as well.

The Art of Spiritual Ignition

Igniting others with the spiritual flame is both an art and a science. It requires the sensitivity of the Holy Spirit combined with the wisdom that comes from understanding how God typically works in human hearts. While every person's journey toward spiritual renewal is unique, there are proven principles that consistently create environments where ignition can occur.

CHAPTER 10: IGNITING OTHERS - PASSING THE FLAME

Creating Hunger

Before someone can be ignited, they must first recognize their need for fire. Many believers have become so accustomed to spiritual coldness that they no longer realize what they are missing. The effective flame-bearer learns how to create holy dissatisfaction with spiritual mediocrity.

This begins with living in such a way that others cannot help but notice the difference. When your joy is unshakable despite circumstances, when your peace remains steady in the midst of chaos, when your love extends even to difficult people, when your faith operates with supernatural power—others begin to hunger for what you possess.

Creating hunger also involves asking penetrating questions that force people to examine their spiritual condition honestly. "When was the last time you felt God's presence in worship?" "What has God been teaching you through His Word lately?" "How has prayer been changing your perspective on life?" These questions, asked with genuine love and interest, often reveal spiritual emptiness that the person had not previously acknowledged.

Modeling the Life

People are not ignited by theological lectures or emotional appeals alone—they are ignited by witnessing authentic transformation in real life. The flame-bearer's most powerful tool for igniting others is their own life lived in consistent demonstration of spiritual renewal.

This modeling happens in both the extraordinary and the ordinary moments of life. Others watch how you respond to unexpected challenges, how you treat service workers, how you handle financial pressure, how you speak about those who have hurt you, how you prioritize your time and resources. These daily demonstrations of spiritual reality often have more impact than any sermon you might preach.

The modeling must be intentional without being artificial. This means living your normal life with heightened awareness that others are watching and learning. It means being willing to share how your faith influences your decisions, how prayer guides your choices, and how Scripture shapes your worldview.

Providing Practical Steps

Many people become hungry for spiritual renewal and are inspired by the model they see in others, but they still do not know how to begin their own journey. The effective flame-bearer learns how to translate spiritual principles into practical steps that others can immediately implement.

This might involve teaching someone how to establish a meaningful prayer routine, guiding them through a method of Scripture study that brings revelation, introducing them to spiritual disciplines that foster intimacy with God, or showing them how to recognize and respond to the Holy Spirit's leading. The key is providing concrete, actionable steps rather than vague spiritual platitudes.

The Contexts for Ignition

God provides various contexts and opportunities for passing the spiritual flame to others. The wise flame-bearer learns to recognize and maximize these divine appointments while also creating intentional environments where ignition is more likely to occur.

CHAPTER 10: IGNITING OTHERS - PASSING THE FLAME

One-on-One Discipleship

Perhaps the most effective context for spiritual ignition is the intimate setting of one-on-one discipleship. This allows for personalized attention, honest vulnerability, and customized guidance that addresses specific needs and questions. Jesus modeled this approach with individuals like Peter, John, and Mary of Bethany, spending concentrated time investing in their spiritual development.

Effective one-on-one discipleship requires commitment from both parties. The flame-bearer commits to consistent investment of time, energy, and spiritual resources. The one being discipled commits to honest participation, faithful application of principles learned, and eventual multiplication by discipling others.

This approach is not about creating dependency but about providing the intensive care needed during the crucial early stages of spiritual renewal. Like a master craftsman training an apprentice, the discipler gradually transfers responsibility while remaining available for guidance and encouragement.

Small Group Environments

Small groups provide a unique context for spiritual ignition because they combine the intimacy necessary for vulnerability with the dynamics of peer interaction and mutual encouragement. When a small group is properly led, it becomes a greenhouse environment where spiritual growth is accelerated and multiplication occurs naturally.

The most effective small groups for spiritual ignition are those that maintain a careful balance between Bible study, prayer, fellowship, and practical application. Members learn from the Word together, share their struggles and victories honestly, pray for one another with faith and expectation, and hold each other accountable for spiritual growth.

Small groups also provide natural opportunities for emerging leaders to develop their gifts in a safe environment. As group members mature spiritually, they can be given increasing responsibility for leading discussions, facilitating prayer times, or mentoring newer members.

Family Discipleship

The family unit represents perhaps the most overlooked context for spiritual ignition in the modern Church. Parents and grandparents who have experienced spiritual renewal carry a unique responsibility and opportunity to pass the flame to the next generation within their own households.

Family discipleship goes far beyond family devotions or bedtime prayers, though these have their place. It involves creating a family culture where spiritual conversations happen naturally, where biblical principles guide decision-making, where prayer is the family's first response to challenges, and where each family member is encouraged to develop their own intimate relationship with God.

This requires intentionality from parents who must model spiritual authenticity while also creating age-appropriate opportunities for their children to encounter God personally. It means family worship times that engage rather than bore, dinner table conversations that explore spiritual topics, and family service projects that demonstrate faith in action.

CHAPTER 10: IGNITING OTHERS - PASSING THE FLAME

Workplace and Community Witness

The flame-bearer recognizes that some of the greatest opportunities for spiritual ignition occur in the everyday contexts of work, neighborhood, and community involvement. These settings provide natural relationships and authentic opportunities to demonstrate the reality of spiritual transformation.

Workplace witness is not about turning every conversation into a sermon or making colleagues uncomfortable with inappropriate evangelistic efforts. Instead, it involves living with such integrity, excellence, and grace that others are compelled to ask about the source of your character and perspective.

Community involvement provides opportunities to serve alongside non-believers in ways that demonstrate the love of Christ practically. Whether through volunteer work, neighborhood associations, or civic engagement, the flame-bearer looks for ways to be salt and light in the broader community.

Overcoming Obstacles to Ignition

Even the most passionate flame-bearer will encounter obstacles and challenges in the process of igniting others. Understanding these common barriers and developing strategies to overcome them is essential for sustained effectiveness in spiritual multiplication.

The Obstacle of Fear

Many believers who have experienced personal spiritual renewal still struggle with fear when it comes to sharing that experience with others.

They fear rejection, ridicule, or their own inadequacy to effectively communicate spiritual truths. This fear often paralyzes them from taking any action toward igniting others.

The antidote to fear is not the elimination of all nervousness or uncertainty, but rather the cultivation of love that becomes stronger than fear. When our concern for others' spiritual condition exceeds our concern for our own comfort or reputation, we find the courage to act despite our fears.

Overcoming fear also requires starting small and building confidence through positive experiences. Rather than attempting to ignite entire crowds, begin with one person who already shows some openness to spiritual things. Success in small settings builds confidence for larger opportunities.

The Obstacle of Impatience

Spiritual ignition rarely happens as quickly as we would like. The flame-bearer must learn to work with God's timing rather than forcing results according to human schedules. This requires the development of patient perseverance that can continue investing in others even when immediate results are not visible.

Impatience often leads to manipulation, pressure tactics, or premature abandonment of relationships that could eventually bear fruit. The effective flame-bearer learns to plant seeds, water them faithfully, and trust God for the increase in His perfect timing.

The Obstacle of Discouragement

CHAPTER 10: IGNITING OTHERS - PASSING THE FLAME

Not everyone who encounters the flame will choose to be ignited. Some will show initial interest but fail to follow through with commitment. Others will resist or even ridicule the message of spiritual renewal. These experiences can tempt the flame-bearer to become discouraged and withdraw from further attempts at ignition.

Overcoming discouragement requires maintaining an eternal perspective that recognizes our responsibility to be faithful rather than successful. Our job is to present the opportunity for spiritual renewal authentically and lovingly; the results belong to God and to the free will choices of those we seek to influence.

The Obstacle of Pride

Perhaps the most dangerous obstacle facing the flame-bearer is the temptation to pride that comes with seeing others respond positively to their influence. When people begin to experience spiritual renewal through our investment, it is easy to begin taking credit for what God alone can accomplish.

Pride not only corrupts the flame-bearer's own spiritual condition but also makes them less effective at igniting others. People are drawn to humility and authenticity, not to spiritual arrogance or self-promotion. The moment we begin to see ourselves as the source of ignition rather than simply the vessel through which God works, our effectiveness diminishes significantly.

The Multiplication Effect

When spiritual ignition is approached with wisdom, patience, and dependence on the Holy Spirit, it creates a multiplication effect that extends far beyond the original flame-bearer's direct influence. Each person who is successfully ignited becomes a potential flame-bearer themselves, creating an exponential expansion of spiritual renewal.

This multiplication effect is what transformed a small band of disciples into a movement that eventually reached the entire known world. It is what fueled the great revivals throughout church history. It is what God desires to accomplish through every believer who takes seriously their calling to pass the flame to others.

The beauty of spiritual multiplication is that it does not depend on extraordinary human abilities or resources. It depends on ordinary people who are willing to be used by an extraordinary God. When we make ourselves available as instruments of ignition, God provides the power, the opportunities, and the results.

A Legacy of Fire

The flame that burns in your heart today carries within it the potential to ignite countless others throughout generations. Every person you influence for spiritual renewal has the potential to influence dozens of others, who in turn influence hundreds more. This is how individual revival becomes corporate awakening, and how personal renewal becomes cultural transformation.

Consider the legacy you want to leave behind. Will you be remembered as someone who hoarded the flame for personal blessing, or as someone who sacrificed comfort and convenience to ensure that others could experience the same transforming fire that changed your own life?

The choice is before you every day in every relationship and interaction.

CHAPTER 10: IGNITING OTHERS - PASSING THE FLAME

The person sitting next to you at work, the neighbor who struggles with discouragement, the family member who has drifted from faith, the friend who searches for meaning—each represents an opportunity to pass the flame.

The spiritual flame that God has entrusted to you is not yours to keep but yours to give. In the divine economy of the Kingdom, the flame grows brighter as it is shared and dimmer when it is hoarded. The very act of igniting others fans your own flame into greater intensity and purity.

May you embrace the sacred privilege and awesome responsibility of being a flame-bearer in this generation. May you live with the constant awareness that someone is watching, learning, and potentially being ignited by the reality of spiritual renewal demonstrated through your life.

The flame awaits passing. The darkness waits to be driven back. Others wait to be ignited. The question that remains is simply this: Will you be faithful to pass the flame?

Chapter 11: A Church in Fire

As we reach the end of our journey together through these pages, we stand at a crossroads that every generation of believers has faced: Will we allow the spiritual flame within the Body of Christ to dim to barely glowing embers, or will we fan it into a consuming fire that transforms not only our own hearts but ignites revival in our communities and beyond?

The path forward is neither simple nor comfortable. Rekindling the spiritual flame requires us to move beyond the superficial trappings of modern Christianity and dive deep into the wellspring of authentic faith that has sustained believers through centuries of triumph and trial. It demands that we confront the complacency that has settled like dust over many of our churches, the entertainment-driven worship that has replaced genuine encounter with the Divine, and the cultural accommodation that has diluted the transformative power of the Gospel.

Yet within these challenges lies unprecedented opportunity. We live in an age when spiritual hunger is palpable, when souls cry out for meaning beyond material success, when hearts long for the authentic community and purpose that only Christ can provide. The very darkness of our

CHAPTER 11: A CHURCH IN FIRE

time creates the perfect backdrop for the light of Christ to shine more brilliantly than ever before.

The spiritual flame we seek to rekindle is not merely about emotional experiences or religious enthusiasm, though these may be part of the journey. Rather, it is about returning to the radical discipleship that marked the early Church—a faith so transformative that it turned the Roman Empire upside down, not through political maneuvering or cultural influence, but through the sheer power of lives completely surrendered to Christ.

This rekindling begins with each individual believer choosing to abandon the comfortable Christianity of casual commitment and embrace the costly grace that demands everything while offering infinitely more in return. It means rediscovering the disciplines of prayer, fasting, Scripture meditation, and corporate worship not as religious duties but as lifelines to the heart of God. It requires us to cultivate intimacy with the Holy Spirit, learning to recognize His voice, follow His leading, and depend on His power rather than our own wisdom and strength.

But individual transformation, while essential, is only the beginning. The spiritual flame burns brightest when it spreads from heart to heart, from believer to believer, creating communities of faith that mirror the love, unity, and power of the Trinity itself. This means breaking down the walls that divide us—denominational barriers, racial prejudices, economic distinctions, and generational misunderstandings—and discovering our profound unity in Christ.

The Church ablaze is a Church that no longer seeks to blend seamlessly into the surrounding culture but stands as a prophetic voice, calling the world to something higher, deeper, and more beautiful than the broken systems that promise much but deliver only emptiness. It is a Church that demonstrates the Kingdom of God not merely through words but through radical acts of love, justice, mercy, and sacrifice that leave observers with no choice but to ask, "What makes these people different?"

As leaders within the Body of Christ, we bear a sacred responsibility to model this rekindled flame. Our preaching must burn with divine fire, our prayers must carry the weight of heaven, our lives must exhibit the fruit of genuine transformation. We cannot give what we do not possess, nor can we lead others to fires we ourselves have never approached. The call to rekindle the spiritual flame in the Church begins with allowing that same flame to consume our own hearts completely.

This is not a call to return to some romanticized version of Christianity's past, but rather a summons to press forward into the fullness of what God intends for His Church in this pivotal moment of history. The challenges we face—secularization, moral relativism, spiritual apathy, and cultural hostility—are not obstacles to be feared but opportunities for the Gospel to demonstrate its power to save, heal, and transform even the most hardened hearts and broken systems.

The rekindled flame will manifest differently in different contexts—in some places as gentle revival, in others as revolutionary awakening. Some communities will experience restoration through renewed worship and discipleship, while others will find their flame fanned through costly obedience in the face of persecution. What remains constant is the source of the flame: the unchanging love of God, the finished work of Christ, and the ongoing ministry of the Holy Spirit.

We stand on the shoulders of countless saints who kept the flame burning through dark ages, persecution, and cultural upheaval. Now the torch has been passed to us. Future generations will judge whether we proved faithful stewards of this sacred trust or allowed it to flicker and die on our watch.

The choice is ours, and the time is now. Will we be content with churches that are merely warm, or will we cry out for the consuming fire of God's presence? Will we settle for religious routine, or will we pursue the wild, unpredictable, transformative power of the Gospel unleashed? Will we remain comfortable in our Christian subculture, or will we allow the love of Christ to compel us into a lost and dying world with the only message that can truly save?

The spiritual flame awaits rekindling. The Church stands ready for revival. The world desperately needs what only the Body of Christ can offer. May we be found faithful to fan the flame until it becomes a blazing fire that illuminates the darkness, warms the cold, and draws all people to the irresistible love of Jesus Christ.

Let the Church be ablaze once more. Let the spiritual flame burn bright. Let this generation be remembered as the one that chose costly obedience over comfortable compromise, radical discipleship over casual Christianity, and the narrow path of authentic faith over the broad road of cultural accommodation.

The flame is in our hands. What will we do with it?

"I have come to bring fire on the earth, and how I wish it were already kindled!" - Luke 12:49

May it be so, Lord Jesus. May it be so.

Prayer for Spiritual Renewal

Heavenly Father, We come before Your throne of grace with hearts that acknowledge our desperate need for spiritual renewal. We confess that we have allowed the flame of our first love to grow dim, and we have settled for the shadows of religion when You have called us to walk in the fullness of Your light.

Lord Jesus Christ, You are the same yesterday, today, and forever. You are the One who baptizes with the Holy Spirit and with fire. We cry out to You as the church in Laodicea should have cried—recognizing that we are wretched, pitiful, poor, blind, and naked without Your transforming presence. Come and sup with us. Open the door that we have kept closed through our self-sufficiency and spiritual pride.

Holy Spirit, You are the Promise of the Father, the One who brings conviction, comfort, and power. We invite You to move among us as You did in the upper room, as You did through the early church, as You have done in every true revival throughout history. Search our hearts and reveal every area where we have grieved You through compromise, apathy, or rebellion.

We confess:

- Our lukewarm devotion when You deserve passionate worship
  - Our prayerless days when You long for intimate communion
  - Our self-reliant efforts when You offer supernatural power
  - Our scattered focus when You call us to seek first Your kingdom
  - Our comfort with the status quo when You desire transformation
  - Our fear of man when we should fear You alone
  - Our love of this world's systems when You have called us to be set

CHAPTER 11: A CHURCH IN FIRE

apart

Forgive us, Lord, for we have sinned against You in thought, word, and deed. We have left our first love and pursued other gods—the gods of success, comfort, approval, and security. Wash us clean with the blood of Jesus and create in us pure hearts that burn with holy passion for Your glory alone.

We cry out for renewal:

Renew our minds that we might think Your thoughts and see with Your perspective. Transform us by Your Word until our worldview aligns perfectly with Your truth.

Renew our hearts that we might love what You love and hate what You hate. Give us hearts of flesh that are tender toward You and broken for the lost.

Renew our spirits that we might walk in step with Your Spirit, sensitive to Your voice, and quick to obey Your promptings.

Renew our churches that they might become houses of prayer for all nations, centers of transformative worship, and launching pads for Your kingdom advancement.

Renew our families that our homes might become sanctuaries where Your presence dwells and training grounds where the next generation learns to walk with You.

Renew our communities that Your light might shine through us into the darkness, bringing hope to the hopeless and salvation to the lost.

Father, we ask for:

A spirit of prayer and supplication that drives us to our knees in desperation for Your presence and power. May our churches become houses of prayer where intercession flows like a river and worship ascends like incense.

A hunger for Your Word that surpasses our desire for daily bread. Give us hearts that crave the pure milk and solid food of Scripture, and minds that meditate on Your truth day and night.

Unity in the Body of Christ that transcends denominational boundaries, racial divisions, and generational gaps. May we be one as You and Jesus are one, that the world might believe.

Boldness to proclaim the Gospel with power, signs, and wonders following. Remove the spirit of fear and timidity, and clothe us with divine courage to speak Your truth in love.

Compassion for the lost that breaks our hearts as it breaks Yours. Give us eyes to see people as You see them—precious souls for whom Christ died, wandering in darkness and desperately needing the light of the Gospel.

Wisdom to discern the times and know what Your Church should do in this critical hour of history. Help us to be faithful stewards of the mysteries of God and watchful guardians of the Gospel.

Lord, we specifically pray for:

Our pastors and leaders—anoint them afresh with Your Spirit. Give them

CHAPTER 11: A CHURCH IN FIRE

vision, courage, and unwavering commitment to Your truth. Protect them from discouragement, compromise, and the schemes of the enemy.

Our young people —capture their hearts with a vision of Your glory that eclipses the temporary pleasures of this world. Raise up a generation that will not bow to the idols of their age but will stand firm in the faith.

Our families—heal the broken relationships, restore the prodigals, and establish homes built on the solid foundation of Your Word and saturated with Your presence.

Our nation and the nations—send revival that begins in Your house and spreads to every corner of the earth. May Your kingdom come and Your will be done on earth as it is in heaven.

We surrender everything to You:

Our plans and dreams, our resources and abilities, our reputation and comfort, our very lives—all of it belongs to You. We acknowledge that we are not our own; we have been bought with a price. Use us as vessels of honor, sanctified and useful for the Master's work.

Come, Holy Spirit, with convicting power that leads to repentance, with comforting grace that heals the brokenhearted, and with consuming fire that purifies and empowers Your Church.

Come, Lord Jesus, and manifest Your presence among us. Let Your glory fill this place as the waters cover the sea. May Your name be hallowed, Your kingdom come, and Your will be done in our hearts, in our churches, and in our world.

We make this prayer in the mighty name of Jesus Christ, who gave Himself as a ransom for many, who was raised for our justification, and who ever lives to make intercession for the saints.

Amen and Amen.

"If my people, who are called by my name, will humble themselves and pray and seek my face and turn from their wicked ways, then I will hear from heaven, and I will forgive their sin and will heal their land." - 2 Chronicles 7:14

"Will you not revive us again, that your people may rejoice in you?" - Psalm 85:6

Conclusion

It becomes clear that the spiritual flame within the Body of Christ is not merely a metaphor—it is the very life force that sustains, empowers, and transforms the Church in every generation. This flame, kindled by the Holy Spirit at Pentecost, has burned through centuries of triumph and trial, persecution and prosperity, always finding a way to illuminate the darkness and warm the hearts of those who seek God with genuine faith.

The question that has guided our exploration is not whether this flame exists—it burns eternal in the heart of the Almighty—but whether we, as individual believers and as the collective Body of Christ, will position ourselves to receive its transforming power. Will we clear away the debris of complacency, the ashes of past disappointments, and the damp wood of spiritual compromise that threatens to smother the very fire we desperately need?

Throughout this book, we have examined the symptoms of spiritual decline that plague too many congregations today: prayer meetings with empty chairs, worship that lacks authentic encounter, believers who know doctrine but lack devotion, and churches that have programs but no power. Yet we have also discovered that these conditions are not terminal diagnoses but rather invitations to return to the Source of all spiritual vitality.

The rekindling of the spiritual flame requires both individual and corporate response. It demands that we personally cultivate intimacy with God through prayer, meditation on His Word, and surrender to His will. It calls us to fast from the distractions that fragment our attention and feast instead on the presence of the Living God. It requires that we confess not only our personal sins but also our corporate lukewarmness, our tendency to substitute human effort for divine empowerment, and our willingness to settle for spiritual mediocrity.

But personal revival, while essential, is incomplete without corporate transformation. The flame burns brightest when believers gather with expectant hearts, united in purpose, and hungry for God's presence. It spreads most rapidly when churches prioritize prayer over programs, when leadership models authentic spirituality rather than mere administration, and when the Body of Christ functions as an organism rather than an organization.

The obstacles we face are real but not insurmountable. Cultural pressures, institutional traditions, and personal preferences will always challenge our pursuit of spiritual authenticity. However, history teaches us that God delights in using ordinary people who are willing to pay the price for extraordinary spiritual breakthrough. He has done it before, and He will do it again—but only through those who are willing to abandon themselves completely to His purposes.

As you close this book and return to your daily life, remember that the spiritual flame is not something you must create—it already exists within you if you are a believer. Your task is to remove the barriers that prevent it from burning brightly and to position yourself where the wind of the Spirit can fan it into a consuming fire. This may require uncomfortable changes in your schedule, your priorities, and your commitments. It may demand that you distance yourself from relationships and activities that quench the Spirit and draw closer to those that fuel your spiritual passion.

The stakes could not be higher. A world lost in darkness desperately needs to see the light of Christ burning brightly in His people. A generation marked by despair needs to witness the hope that comes from genuine encounter with the living God. A society fragmented by division needs to observe the unity that flows from hearts transformed by the same Spirit.

The choice before us is clear: we can continue with business as usual, maintaining religious forms while lacking spiritual power, or we can pay the price for authentic revival in our own hearts and churches. We can remain satisfied with the embers of past moves of God, or we can seek the fresh fire that He desires to pour out in our generation.

The spiritual flame in the Body of Christ is not dying—it is waiting to be rekindled. It waits for hearts hungry enough to seek it, humble enough to receive it, and bold enough to let it burn away everything that is not of God. It waits for believers who will stop making excuses and start making sacrifices, who will cease playing church and start being the Church.

May God find us among those who fan the flame rather than quench it, who kindle revival rather than resist it, and who become the very answer to our own prayers for spiritual awakening. The flame is ready. The question remains: are we?

The fire of God is falling. Let it fall on us.

About the Author

Elou Fleurine is a devoted servant of Christ, dedicated to guiding the Church back to its biblical roots and fostering true spiritual renewal. He is the Senior Pastor Of King Jesus Universal Ministry under the covering of Apostle Guillermo Maldonado. With a heart that burns for revival and a deep love for the Body of Christ, ELOU has dedicated his ministry to calling believers back to authentic discipleship and transformative faith.

Drawing from years of pastoral ministry, biblical study, and firsthand experience with the challenges facing the modern Church, ELOU writes with both prophetic urgency and pastoral compassion. His ministry has been characterized by a commitment to preaching the uncompromising Word of God while demonstrating the love and grace that draws hearts to genuine repentance and renewal.

ELOU's journey into ministry began through a personal encounter with the transforming power of God that radically changed their life and ignited a passion for seeing others experience the same spiritual awakening. This foundational experience continues to fuel a ministry marked by authenticity, biblical fidelity, and an unrelenting pursuit of God's presence.

Throughout the ministry, ELOU has served in various capacities within the Church, gaining invaluable insights into both the struggles and the potential that exist within the modern Body of Christ. Whether preaching from the pulpit, counseling the brokenhearted, or interceding for revival, ELOU has consistently demonstrated a heart that beats in rhythm with God's desire to see His people walk in the fullness of his calling.

With a deep understanding of church history and the movements of God throughout the ages, ELOU brings both historical perspective and contemporary relevance to the urgent need for spiritual renewal in our time. His teaching and writing consistently point believers toward the cross of Christ as the source of true transformation and the foundation upon which genuine revival must be built.

In "Rekindling the Spiritual Flame in the Body of Christ," ELOU combines theological depth with practical application, scholarly insight with pastoral heart. The book reflects years of study, prayer, and ministry experience, offering readers not merely intellectual understanding but a roadmap toward genuine spiritual transformation.

ELOU's personal life reflects the same commitment to authenticity and spiritual depth that characterizes their public ministry. As someone who has experienced both the heights of spiritual breakthrough and the valleys of spiritual struggle, ELOU writes from a place of genuine understanding and hard-won wisdom.

His ministry extends beyond writing to include preaching, teaching, mentoring young ministers, and interceding for revival in the Church. ELOU is particularly burdened for the next generation of believers, recognizing that the future of the Church depends upon raising up disciples who are unwilling to compromise the truth of the Gospel for the sake of cultural acceptance.

Above all, ELOU Fleurine is known as someone who carries a burden for genuine revival in the Church. This is not merely a theological concept or ministerial focus, but a consuming passion that shapes every aspect of life and ministry. ELOU believes deeply that God desires to pour out His Spirit in unprecedented ways in our generation, and that the Church must prepare itself through repentance, prayer, and renewed commitment to biblical truth.

As the Church faces unprecedented challenges in an increasingly secular and hostile culture, ELOU continues to sound the call for believers to return to their first love and rediscover the transformative power of authentic Christianity. Through continued writing, preaching, and ministry, ELOU remains committed to seeing the spiritual flame rekindled in individual hearts and corporate bodies until the Church once again becomes the powerful, prophetic voice God intended it to be.

"Rekindling the Spiritual Flame in the Body of Christ" represents not just ELOU's theological convictions, but the cry of a heart that refuses to accept anything less than the fullness of God's purposes for His people. It is the author's prayer that this book will serve as a catalyst for the kind of spiritual renewal that transforms not only individual lives but entire communities, nations, and ultimately, the world.

www.ingramcontent.com/pod-product-compliance
Lightning Source LLC
Chambersburg PA
CBHW050655160426
43194CB00010B/1943